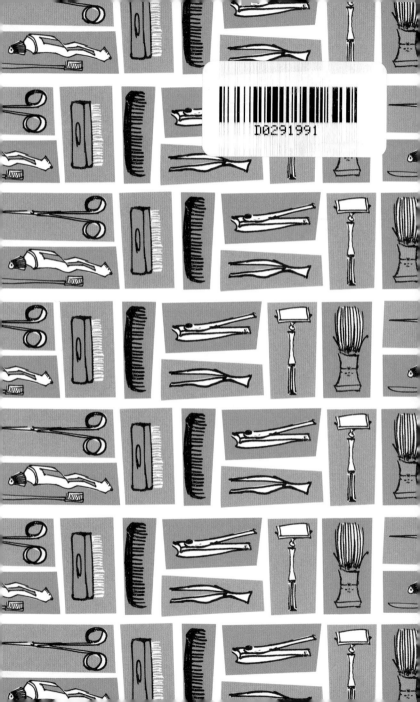

The Perfectly Groomed Gentleman

The Perfectly Groomed Gentleman

Robert O'Byrne

Illustration by Lord Dunsby

CICO BOOKS

LONDON NEW YORK

Published in 2013 by CICO Books
An imprint of Ryland Peters & Small Ltd

20–21 Jockey's Fields   519 Broadway, 5th Floor
London WC1R 4BW   New York, NY 10012

www.rylandpeters.com

10 9 8 7 6 5 4 3 2 1

Text © Robert O'Byrne 2013
Design and illustration © CICO Books 2013

A CIP catalog record for this book is
available from the Library of Congress
and the British Library.

ISBN: 978 1 78249 060 9

Printed in China

Editor: Pete Jorgensen
Design: Jerry Goldie
Illustration: Lord Dunsby aka Steve Millington

For digital editions, visit www.cicobooks.com/apps.php

Contents

Introduction

Should you find yourself engaged in a debate over
the definition of a gentleman, remember that our
current understanding of the nomenclature dates
back only a few hundred years. The word itself
derives from the Latin adjective *gentilis*, meaning
"of or belonging to the same family, group, or race."
Such a notion of the gentleman emerged during
the later Middle Ages. At that time, however, a
gentleman was someone permitted, and even
required, to bear arms in defense of king and
country. In other words, he belonged to an elite
warrior caste, and both his appearance and
manners were of secondary importance.

———◆———

This is certainly not our own understanding of what
constitutes a gentleman. Instead, the modern interpretation
appeared during the Renaissance era, specifically in the
princely courts of Europe, where the wealthy and well bred
were expected to be in attendance on their sovereign and
competed for royal attention, not least through a display of
personal refinement.

Various manuals began to be published during this period
to help would-be gentlemen achieve success in what was a
highly competitive environment. One of the earliest and

unquestionably the most influential of these was Baldassare Castiglione's *Il Libro del Cortegiano* (The Book of the Courtier), which appeared in 1528. His work not only advised on skill at arms but also provided abundant pointers on how best to behave in civil society. Castiglione lived in and wrote for the court of Duke Guidobaldo da Montefeltro in Urbino, a small Italian principality. This, it has been observed, was perhaps the most civilized city of the period. So, for example, one commentator on Castiglione's text has pointed out that Urbino's courtiers were counseled on the necessity of cleanliness, "with particular injunctions as to frequent ablutions, and extraordinary precautions against the unpleasant effects of hot weather on their persons and clothing; in case of need, medical attention is enjoined to correct the breath."

That a gentleman's body should be at all times clean and well groomed took some time to be widely understood,

especially in those parts of Europe not customarily basking in Italian sunshine. Washing tended to be infrequent at a time when filling a tub with hot water took considerably longer than it does today. It was easier for men to go without and to mask inevitable resultant body odors with perfume. Unlike our own era, for millennia the popularity of scent derived from its ability to cover obnoxious smells, many of them produced by humanity. Gradually, however, as the population of cities grew, so did an appreciation of basic hygiene, if only to avoid the spread of disease and infection. Grooming oneself became an act of civility toward others, and so it remains today. Three centuries after Castiglione, that great dandy George "Beau" Brummell could proclaim,

"No perfumes… but very fine linen, plenty of it, and country washing." Quite what he meant by country washing and whether it was intended for clothes or the body beneath is unclear, although we do know that he astounded his contemporaries by washing his entire body daily, an activity hitherto unconsidered even among the wealthiest strata of English society.

Owing to advances made during the Industrial Revolution, it is much easier now for all of us to follow Brummell's example. These developments ensure that in our homes we have an abundant supply of both water, thanks to plumbing, and the chance to heat it, thanks to electricity. In fact, there is no excuse for us not to do both, if only because such opportunities were denied to our ancestors who had to go to a lot more trouble to stay clean. It is like universal suffrage in Western democracies: we have a duty to vote in political elections since the chance to do so is frequently denied elsewhere around the world.

Failure to take advantage of abundant hot water, and thereby keep ourselves clean, is churlish and runs counter to the behavior of other living creatures. Many animal species engage in grooming, either by themselves or helping each other in the process. There is an instinctive understanding that keeping clean is necessary for good health and hygiene. Ornithologists have noticed how much time birds spend grooming themselves, primarily through preening their feathers so as to remove any parasites and keep themselves in sound aerodynamic condition. Cats are also renowned for the amount of time they spend licking themselves clean, with the result that the fur they swallow forms hairballs.

Primates are especially fond of social grooming, a practice whereby members of the same species keep each other clean and thereby form bonds. While we humans do not pick lice from the hair of family and friends, our personal grooming habits do help to bind us to one another: you're less likely to engage in conversation with someone who is obviously unclean. This is why a gentleman should always make sure he is well groomed. It is evidence that he is aware of the people around him, and takes their concerns into account. To paraphrase a well-known proverb, cleanliness is next to neighborliness.

There is an instinctive understanding that keeping clean is necessary for good health and hygiene

When it comes to personal appearance, for the past half-century there have been arguments made against conformity on the grounds of freedom of expression. This line of reasoning has often been advanced when it comes to grooming, whether concerning the length of hair or the display of tattoos. But such an apologia will find no favor with gentlemen who appreciate not just that there are other, better ways to express character than via a well-inked arm but also that we are part of a broader society and its interests surpass our own. No man, John Donne famously pronounced, is an island, and the truth of his observation is invariably recognized by a gentleman. Unless you are Robinson Crusoe, and therefore marooned on your own island, you must interact with the world, and in doing so

present yourself to others in the best possible way. Being well groomed is an integral part of this.

There are other reasons for taking care of yourself, not least that by doing so you are likely to enjoy excellent health, feel well, and have more energy and gusto than would otherwise be the case.

"Better keep yourself clean and bright," George Bernard Shaw once remarked. "You are the window through which you must see the world."

There is an old maxim, used in relation to clothes, that keep clean is better than make clean. The same truth is relevant to our bodies: keeping them fresh on a daily basis is better and involves less effort than trying to make them so after a period of neglect. Good grooming habits are easy to acquire and easy to maintain. But make sure they are invisible to everyone else. Although your grooming regime may demand time and effort, the final result should appear entirely natural: you want to be complimented for looking well, not criticized for displaying vanity. Discretion must be the better part of your valiant work.

While the final definition of a gentleman is probably going to remain open to debate indefinitely, one point on which universal agreement has long been reached is that anybody worthy of the title will always display concern for others. You can do this by keeping yourself clean and smart at all times, with the bonus that you, too, will benefit from the enterprise. Being well groomed is an essential attribute for any gentleman.

Chapter 1

Your Face

Lest you weren't aware, skin is your body's largest organ, covering and protecting everything that lies beneath. Skin is composed of three layers, the lowest one being the subcutaneous layer, which is mostly composed of fat and helps us to keep warm and absorb shocks. It is also where hair production begins. Next comes the dermis containing nerve endings, blood vessels, oil glands, and sweat glands, together with collagen and elastin. Finally, there is the part that we see, the epidermis at the base of which new skin cells form before they rise to the top where they die and are eventually shed, sometimes of their own accord, sometimes aided by processes like shaving. The epidermis is reasonably thick on certain parts of the body, like the soles of your feet and palms of your hands, but becomes thinnest on areas of your face, being just 0.0020 inches deep on the eyelids. You will, therefore, want to give particular care to these places if you want to make sure your skin stays in the best possible condition.

———◆———

While your face, like your DNA, is unique to you, there are certain characteristics it will share with that of other men. The first of these is that it is different from women's skin. Due to the presence of greater levels of male sex hormones known as androgens, of which testosterone is the best known, a man's skin is about 25 per cent thicker than that of a woman and is thus tougher. It is also firmer, thanks to the presence of greater quantities of collagen and elastin, two naturally occurring proteins. Collagen content is directly related to signs of skin aging, which is why men can sometimes look younger than women of the same age. On the other hand, hitherto most males have been less concerned than their female contemporaries with resisting the visible signs of aging or with using protection against sun damage (of which more later) and so the gender age gap is usually not apparent.

These are the obvious advantages enjoyed by male skin. The principal drawback is that toughness leads to coarseness, with higher levels of testosterone production creating larger pores and more active sebaceous glands. This, in turn, means men are more prone to oiliness, blemishes, and clogged pores, and have a greater inclination to sweat.

Late nights, regular consumption of alcohol (which dehydrates) and nicotine, poor diet, lack of sleep, stress, and sun exposure: these factors all take a toll on your skin and require countermeasures. In fact, one simple but effective—and cheap—way of helping your skin look well is to drink sufficient quantities of water. But you cannot and should not take your skin for granted. Instead, you must treat it with the consideration it deserves.

While the situation has changed of late, traditionally men were disinclined to display much interest in caring for their skin, just as they showed little concern in managing their health. Particularly in relation to the avoidance of conditions like skin cancer, this is not a question of vanity but simple common sense. Nevertheless, getting that message across has been a slow process and there are still plenty of men who believe their masculinity would be called into question if they were discovered applying a sunscreen to their faces.

Taking care of your skin

A regular skin regime is highly recommended, starting with thoroughly cleansing your face twice daily. Although your skin is tougher than that of women, it is still vulnerable to aggressive cleansing. Choose a mild, soap-free cleanser; soap can strip skin of essential oils, leaving it dry and raw. After application, rinse until all the cleanser is removed using warm, but not hot water; the latter is too harsh on the skin. Pat your face dry (don't rub) with a clean towel, preferably not the same one you use after emerging from the bathtub or shower, and make sure your skin is completely free of residual moisture.

Once or twice a week, you might consider exfoliation, which is the removal of old dead cells lying on the skin's outermost surface and has been common practice since the time of the Pharaohs. In any pharmacy, you will be able to find a variety of abrasive products on offer, which usually go by the generic title of skin scrub. As with your cleanser, choose one that contains as few chemicals as possible and is not too aggressive (rubbing a tiny amount between your fingers will let you know if this is going to be the case). You only want to wash away the dead surface skin, not drill down to the subcutaneous layer, so be gentle in application. The benefit is clearer skin, with the likelihood of fewer clogged pores and blemishes.

Although, as a rule, men's skin is oilier than that of women, a number of factors can leave your face, or at least parts of it, feeling dry and sore. This may be caused by air conditioning or central heating, or it may be because of a reaction to shaving; the number of possible explanations is infinite. However, the number of solutions is singular: the application of a decent moisturizer that will help increase the skin's level of hydration. It is now commonly accepted that men should moisturize in order to maintain and even improve their skin's condition. Practically every drugstore, pharmacy, and supermarket has a section dedicated to men's grooming, where you will find a number of inexpensive moisturizers, one of which will suit you. Take a bit of time to ascertain the type of moisturizer that is right for your specific skin, and particularly look out for products that are both light in formula and oil-free: these will be more quickly absorbed and not leave residual shine. And it is best to opt for a brand that's fragrance-free, since some perfumes are inclined to cause irritation to sensitive skin. You can apply moisturizer every morning and night; by doing the latter, you give your skin a clear run of seven or eight hours in which to enjoy the benefits. But if you are using a moisturizer before going to bed, why not apply one without a sun protection factor (SPF)—it's not very likely you are going to suffer from sun damage while asleep.

You may wish to apply a separate cream to the most delicate area around your eyes, one specifically created for this purpose, since a moisturizer intended for the rest of your face will not serve.

Protection from the sun

Many moisturizers make claims about their abilities to counter the visible signs of aging. How much any one product can accomplish in this respect is open to question, and scientists tend to be sceptical about whether topical application can penetrate below the epidermis with real sustained effect. What cannot be disputed are the merits of wearing a moisturizer with a high sun protection factor— at the very minimum factor 15 but preferably closer to 30. While your skin needs a certain amount of Vitamin D to stay healthy, as far as possible you should avoid exposure to direct sun during the key hours of 10am to 3pm.

Of late, skin cancer is the cancer men are most likely to experience: in 2008, the American Academy of Dermatology reported that of all the people likely to die annually from melanoma (the most lethal form of skin cancer) 64 percent would be

men. At the same time, almost 50 percent of the men surveyed announced that they never used a sun screen moisturizer, thereby leaving themselves vulnerable to developing skin cancer. This scenario is changing as awareness campaigns become more effective and ever more families are directly affected by skin cancer. However, men remain at greater risk than women and will continue to be until they all take necessary precautions. An SPF moisturizer should be applied daily and not just during sunny weather; you are at risk from skin damage and cancers like melanoma throughout the year. Certainly, you ought never to expose skin to the sun's rays without first applying ample protection, and then regularly reapplying it.

Getting older

Hair grows where?!

Mornings as a young man

Regardless of how much care you take of yourself and your skin, you will grow older. One sign of this advance in years is the unexpected—and unattractive—appearance of hair in places it never grew before and in quantities you never imagined possible. Suddenly tufts start sprouting from your ears and nostrils, and, as if that wasn't bad enough, your eyebrows grow to resemble bat wings. You must act as soon as you see the first signs of these unhappy developments, which frequently coincide with the permanent departure of hair where you most want to retain it: on top of your head. Keep your eyebrows in check by clipping them with fine scissors every couple of days. Don't pluck your eyebrows: you risk looking like Joan Crawford in one of her hammier roles. Any decent pharmacy will sell you a small electrical device specifically designed to trim the hair in your ears and

Mornings as an older gentleman

nostrils, again something that will require attention several times a week. Don't allow these outbreaks of hirsuteness get out of control; they are one of the most obvious, but also most easily managed, indications of aging.

Nip and tuck

As a rule, men find growing older, and displaying evidence of same, less troublesome than do women. However, increasing numbers of men would rather look younger, or at least better, than might be the case if they did not stage an intervention. In addition to using moisturizer and avoiding the sun, these men feel the need to seek professional help. In 2006, *Forbes* magazine reported that over the previous five years, minimally invasive cosmetic procedures for men had increased by 44 percent, while Botox applications had grown over the same period by 233 percent.

With regard to the former, the most popular type of cosmetic surgery for men is not on their faces but involves liposuction to remove fat from their bodies (and, increasingly, from their breasts as more and more men seem to be developing what have become popularly known as "moobs"). But among facial surgery options, rhinoplasty (remodeling of

More and more men seem to be developing what has become popularly know as "moobs"

noses) and tucks either below the eyes or of eyelids, as well as complete lifts attract ever-greater numbers of consumers. As for Botox, this is a highly toxic substance, as indicated by the product's full name, Botulinum Toxin. When injected into the dermis, it paralyzes the muscle and thereby gives a superficial appearance of youth that lasts for six months on average.

So, should you give consideration to either cosmetic surgery or Botox? Neither is cheap and neither is permanent. Both delay signs of aging but cannot deter them forever. And this is perhaps the greatest drawback to engaging in such practices: they have to be repeated if you want to sustain the results. The world is full of cosmetic surgery and Botox junkies, addicted to having procedures intended to give them the appearance of youth. There are, however, certain parts of the anatomy that are unable to be treated in this way—the neck and upper arms, for example—and which, no matter how young-looking is the face above, always betray a person's true age. Another downside to these procedures is that not only do they remove signs of age but also of character: the greater the amount of surgery or Botox undertaken, the less sense of an individual remains.

If you are determined to undertake one or other, or both, of these lines of action, do so in full awareness of the consequence, which is that sooner or later your attempt to defy time will be defeated. And insist that the medical professional who treats you approaches the task with the lightest of touches. The outcome of any work ought to leave you looking fresh, not static or unnaturally sprightly. All of us have seen victims of excessive surgical intervention, left with expressions of perpetual surprise and eyebrows apparently attempting to reach the crown of their skulls. Likewise, people who have overdosed on Botox and could no longer register surprise or alarm even if told their houses had just burned to the ground. Let your faces reflect your experience and the life you have known until now, not some artificial standard of youth.

Blemishes

Unfortunately, male skin has larger pores and is prone to greater oiliness than female skin. As a result, many men suffer from blemishes such as blackheads and acne. One way to minimize the likelihood of these conditions, or to keep them under control, is to follow the skin regime outlined previously on pages 17–19. On the other hand, there are times when greater intervention is required than just regular cleansing and exfoliation.

Acne and other so-called skin blemishes are most prevalent among teenagers whose hormones are especially active. However, this kind of condition is by no means exclusive to puberty and can be more discomforting for adults precisely because it is less common. Beneath the skin surface, a fatty substance called sebum empties into our hair follicles. When it gets stuck, as can sometimes occur, the backup produces what is known as a whitehead: if it is stuck on the surface of the skin and exposed to air, oxygenation will turn it into a blackhead. Once more sebum backs up, pressure grows on the surrounding skin, leaving it red and inflamed. This, simply explained, is acne.

There is nothing "dirty" about blemished skin—the majority of people with acne are, in fact, zealous about cleansing—but Western culture tends to view it as rather unattractive. Because we place a high premium on clear skin, acne is especially unfortunate. It also usually treatable, so there is no need for anyone who has the condition not to find a cure. There are lots of products available in drugstores and pharmacies, and one of these ought to do the job. If not, then it is worth seeing a doctor or dermatologist who will be able to prescribe retinol-based creams and gels designed to produce clear skin. Retinol is a form of Vitamin A, the topical application of which has been shown to clear acne. Don't put up with blemished skin. It can be easily and speedily banished and you will be the beneficiary.

Chapter 2

Shaving and Facial Hair

Shaving is an activity that literally separates the men from the boys, and from the opposite sex, too. For most of us, it's a daily activity, one of the rituals of our morning preparation. It has been estimated that the average man will shave 20,000 times during his life, spending around three and a half minutes a day, which adds up to around 900 hours in the 60 years between ages 15 and 75. Over that period, in the region of 27 feet (over eight meters) of hair will be removed, most of it washed down a sink (and you wonder why these sometimes become blocked).

———◆———

Shaving

Given the statistics, you would think that most men will soon learn how to shave properly, but evidence indicates otherwise. Somehow many of us demonstrate that practice doesn't always make perfect: we shave every day, but consistently mess it up.

A few useful tips about shaving:

• Consider using a shaving brush made from badger hair. Yes, it adds time to the procedure, but there are advantages: the bristle holds a lot of water, producing a richer lather which in turn ensures less dragging on the skin. Additionally, a brush acts as a gentle exfoliant on your face, removing dead skin cells prior to shaving.

• Whether you opt for a cream or a gel (the latter is often deemed preferable because it helps a blade glide over the skin and is less liable to clog pores), use a product that contains glycerine, since this lubricates and protects. Products containing alcohol, mint or menthol, or other fragrances should be avoided: these can sometimes cause a reaction to skin, which is particularly vulnerable after being shaved.

• Prepare your razor by allowing it to soak for a few seconds in hot water; you'll notice the benefits immediately. Change your blade regularly; every week is recommended. Blades not only become dull with age but also more susceptible to a buildup of residue, which can lead to skin infection.

• If you cut yourself, staunch the bleeding and then apply a styptic pencil (available from drugstores and pharmacies), to stop the blood flowing and also prevent infection.

• After shaving, always apply a balm or moisturizer. This should be unperfumed—the chemicals in some products can cause an allergic reaction on freshly shaven skin—but, ideally, should contain an antiseptic to assist in closing pores and preventing infection.

• Electric razors are preferred by some men, but seemingly some 85 percent of the world's males would sooner experience a wet shave. On the other hand, you ought to own an electric razor: it is invaluable for tidying up any tufts of hair overlooked while wet-shaving or for running over the face on evenings when you have an engagement and want to look your best.

• Anybody with curly hair will know the problem of in-growing hair. One of the best solutions is to soak a face cloth or flannel in hot water and hold this over the afflicted area for a short period. Then use a pair of sterilized tweezers to pluck out the hair causing the problem. Pat the skin dry and apply a little moisturizer.

A couple more statistics: the average man's face contains anything between 5,000 and 25,000 whiskers but, regardless of number, they all tend to grow at the same rate—around half an inch per month (or six inches a year). Keeping so many of the little blighters in check is not a straightforward task, which helps to explain why Mr. Average's skills in this area are limited.

Luckily, these skills can easily be improved, not least by taking a bit more time and trouble over the task. Rush the job and you are likely to botch it. Schedule just five more minutes than has hitherto been the case for your daily shave and you will experience immediate results—not only an improved appearance but also greater facial comfort because one of the drawbacks to sloppy shaving is physical pain, owing to the increased likelihood of blemishes, nicks, and rawness. Avoid all these hazards by learning how to shave properly. You'll find minimal effort repays with maximum results.

Facial hair

After puberty, all men have facial hair, albeit of differing density and strength—some men find the bottom half of their faces enveloped in thick dark hair, while others will manage only patchy coverage at best. How much or how little of this you want to leave on display is a matter of choice, although if your hair growth is light, then remaining clean-shaven is probably best: there's something rather inadequate about a wispy beard.

How to Shave Properly

1. Soften the hair on your face, either by splashing it with warm water or by covering it with a warm, damp cloth for a minute or so.

2. If you're susceptible to post-shave rash (and even if not), apply a few drops of pre-shave oil. This will further soften up the skin.

3. Cover the lower section of your face and neck with shaving cream, ideally applied with a badger-hair brush. This will help to build up a rich lather and lift up each whisker.

4. Begin by shaving first one cheek, then the other, down as far as the jaw line and an inch either side of your mouth. Shave with or across—not against—the grain of your beard, as this is the best way to avoid irritation. Shave in short strokes and constantly rinse your blade in clean water.

5. Next shave your neck, again making sure not to run the blade against the beard grain. Finally, tackle around your chin, and below and above your mouth.

6. Once completely shaved, splash with water and then check if any areas have been missed. Once you are clean-shaven, close the pores with plenty of cold water and then pat the skin dry. Finally, but essentially, conclude with the application of a thin layer of moisturizer.

Beards

Beards can be grown for religious reasons (as is the case for Sikhs, who are also forbidden to cut the hair on their heads). In many ancient civilizations, a beard was deemed evidence of strength and virility but it could also serve as a form of decoration. In Egypt under the Pharaohs, for example, the highest caste of men wore hair on their chin, which could be dyed with henna or interwoven with gold thread. And the Pharaohs themselves wore a false metal beard as a sign of sovereignty. However, from the time of Alexander the Great onward, the Greeks and then the Romans preferred to be

As a rule, women don't like beards. At the same time, other men judged beards made their wearers appear more dignified

clean-shaven, regarding beards as evidence of slovenliness: Hadrian was the first Roman Emperor to have worn a beard (seemingly grown to hide facial scars). Early Christians, with their customary habit of going against the popular vote, approved of beards since shaving was indicative of personal vanity, which is why all the first saints and martyrs tend to be shown with luxuriant growth on their chins.

Since then beards have gone in and out of fashion, the last time they were widespread in Europe and the United States being the second half of the 19th century, when full, heavy beards and side-whiskers were hugely popular. Then, in the years after World War I, the clean-shaven face returned to vogue and has remained the preference of the majority ever since. Beards made a reappearance in the 1960s as part of the counter-culture movement, especially among hippies, but they never attained universal support. Such remains the case today: most men shave. On the other hand, daily shaving is tiresome and time-consuming, and for some men also painful. Therefore the alternative option of growing a beard can be appealing.

If you do want to go down this route, just bear in mind the following points:

1. It is sometimes suggested that a beard acts as a form of disguise and therefore implies the wearer has something to hide, or is less trustworthy. It is possible that unconsciously all of us assume a bearded man is engaged in some kind of concealment. And there is a widespread urban legend that men with beards are more likely to be stopped at airport security checkpoints because they arouse suspicion.

2. One might also add that, as a rule, women don't like beards (they make a man's face itchy, apparently). An academic study conducted in New Zealand in 2012 found that women considered men with beards less attractive. At the same time, other men judged beards made their wearers appear more dignified. So, which would you rather have: your dignity or your girl?

3. Beards are prohibited in a number of professions. They are currently not allowed in any branch of the US Military, for example, although some moustaches are still permitted. Sometimes there is a sound reason for the ban: firefighters and airline pilots, for example, need to be clean-shaven to allow for a gas or oxygen mask to fit perfectly to their faces. In other instances, as with members of the armed or police forces in many states, the rule seems dictated primarily by a desire for the workforce to present a uniformly tidy appearance. If you insist on wearing a beard, this may influence your choice of profession.

4. Don't make the mistake of imagining that a beard requires no maintenance. If you are going to have facial hair, then you ought to keep it tidy. This means shaving the lower part of your neck, from around the Adam's apple down, so that it doesn't become populated by straggly hairs, and your beard ends in a clean line instead. And speaking of clean, make sure your beard never acquires evidence of recent food or drink consumption. If we want to know about your last meal, we can ask.

5. You should keep your beard an even length, ideally ensuring it does not grow too long. There are plenty of electrical trimmers, coming with an assortment of attachments, which allow you to keep a beard neat. There's no advantage to keeping the rest of your appearance tidy if your beard then looks a mess.

6. Goatee beards used to be popular among science teachers, who also wore corduroy jackets and knitted wool ties. More recently, the goatee has been discovered by actor Brad Pitt, a handsome man seemingly on a mission to make himself unattractive. There is nothing alluring about the goatee or its sundry variants, like the fulsome Van Dyke or the close-cut circle beard (otherwise known as a door knocker). And a goatee without an accompanying moustache is the facial equivalent of emerging only half-dressed.

7. There was a fashion in the 1980s, fueled by such icons of the era as singer George Michael and the television series *Miami Vice*, for what became known as "designer stubble" (this, incidentally, was a period when the word *designer*, hitherto a little-employed noun, turned into an overworked adjective). Designer stubble is neither a beard, nor is it clean-shaven: it is simply evidence that you have too much time on your hands.

8. The same is true of all facial hair that takes a circuitous route about your cheeks and chin. This kind of beard decoration is popular among young men and takes the form of strips of hair trimmed so thin they could be mistaken for lines drawn with a fountain pen. While the workmanship is undoubtedly impressive, one has to conclude: so much effort to so little purpose.

Additional facial hair

Two other items of facial hair also require brief remarks.

Moustaches

It is rare for a man simply to allow the hair between his upper lip and nose to grow unattended. Inevitably, it is subject to grooming, frequently of the most elaborate sort. Some Indian men, for instance, grow enormous handlebar moustaches of the sort favored by the English actor Jimmy Edwards: the world's widest moustache (14 feet long) is worn by Ram Singh Chauhan of India. Related to this is the pencil-thin-but-extended moustache with curled, waxed tips, which was the trademark of Surrealist artist Salvador Dali. In the past, the pencil moustache tended to be the preserve of suave

The moustache has no function except as a piece of decoration and therefore needs to be idiosyncratic

bounders, chaps like Errol Flynn or David Niven, although of late its best-known advocate is alternative filmmaker John Waters. At the opposite extreme is the type of small moustache favoured by, and now forever associated with, Adolf Hitler—and, before him, Charlie Chaplin.

As the above list will indicate, moustaches are often treated by their wearers as an outlet for self-expression and the establishment of a distinctive identity: a heavy burden to place on a minor outbreak of facial hair. But what other purpose can a moustache serve? It is neither one thing nor the other; it has no function except as a piece of decoration and therefore needs to be idiosyncratic. Grow one if you can discover no other means to convey your unique character, but please keep it tidy and clean. And unless you intend to be mistaken for a pornographic actor from the 1970s, do not allow the ends of your moustache to extend below the edge of your mouth.

Sideburns

For the majority of men, their sideburns take the shape of neat rectangles extending no lower than the earlobe. This is an orderly way to keep a sideburn, signaling the right degree of

virility held in check. *Autres temps, autres mœurs:* during the Napoleonic era, and particularly among members of the military, luxurious side whiskers became the norm. These, in turn, developed into the vast bushy beards widely worn throughout the Victorian era. But when the beards went at the start of the last century, so, too, did the sideburns. They were brought back in the late 1950s and early 1960s as a sign of youthful rebellion, although those developed by Elvis Presley have since acquired a significance that is more ironic than iconic. Depending on your degree of hirsuteness, sideburns, like moustaches, can take whatever form you choose to give them. But the more elaborate that form, the greater amount of attention it will demand. Ultimately, the simplest solution is to keep sideburns short and tidy. You have more constructive ways to pass the day than fiddling with the hair on your cheeks.

Chapter 3

Hair

It was St. Paul, always a reliable source for quotations, who first proclaimed hair a crowning glory. In this instance, he was specifically referring to women, which just goes to prove that Biblical quotes are not necessarily reliable: in the Old Testament's Song of Solomon, for example, the narrator at one point proclaims, "Thy hair is as a flock of goats that appear from Mount Gilead." Most of us have seen men with that kind of bushy hair and it's never an attractive spectacle.

———◆———

Regardless of St. Paul's gender bias, there's no reason why a man's hair should be, if not a crowning glory, then certainly a definite asset. After all, it is likely to be one of the first things people you meet will notice and, whether you like the idea or not, they are liable to judge you by the state of your hair. If it's dirty and/or messy, unfavorable conclusions will be drawn about your character. One way to make a good first impression, therefore, is to keep your hair clean and tidy. That way nobody will have an erroneous opinion of you.

The barber

Like so much else about your appearance, hair should look terrific without indicating anything much has been done to achieve its present superlative condition. Here you have the opportunity to practice the art that conceals art, giving the impression of natural spontaneity despite the time and effort required to achieve this. But even if you're not going to make a lot of effort or spend much time on your hair, abide by the rules of perpetual cleanliness and tidiness, and you'll be fine.

So, above all, make sure you schedule a regular haircut, ideally every month, even if this only entails the ends being trimmed. Why not make a point of having your hair cut on the first Monday or last Saturday or whatever? That way, you will find it easy to remember when it is time to visit the barber.

As for the latter, finding the right barber is like finding the right barman; you might be lucky and get it right first time, or you might have to trawl a lot of joints before coming across the place where you feel at home. Your barber should be not just competent at his job (in the sense that he doesn't send you home with a head full of nicks), but also understand what style works best for you.

In addition, he needs to have some understanding of the human character and appreciate your temperament. This is the trait that barbers share with barmen: the best ones are empathetic and can offer advice whenever it is required. Just as many women like to confide in their hairdresser, so a lot of men like to have personal conversations with their barber, even if it is only to exchange an opinion on the weekend sports results. Any decent barber becomes an amateur therapist as he cuts and shaves, providing customers with an opportunity to discuss whatever topics they wish. On the other hand, if you prefer to have your hair cut in silence, the barber should understand that as well; it helps to bring a newspaper or book when you sit down. Alternatively, keep your eyes closed, although this means you can't see what the barber is doing to your hair.

Once you have established a good relationship with your barber—make sure you tip him at the end of every visit—you can feel free to drop by after a fortnight or so just to have the back of your neck and the area around your ears given a quick trim. It will help to keep your hair neat and means you'll only need to have a full cut once each month. Tidying these areas is a task that takes no more than five minutes but makes all the difference.

One other point: your own high standards of cleanliness should be shared by your barber. Watch that he sterilizes all his equipment and uses a fresh blade when shaving the back of your neck. Otherwise you risk catching an infection passed on from another customer. The barber's premises should also be well maintained, with all hair swept up from the floor after every cut.

Choosing the right style

Like your clothes, you should wear your hair in the style that best suits your features. It is worth taking a little trouble to find out what works for your facial shape and coloring, and then keeping to the same style. Not all men look good with very short hair, while few of us can carry off long hair, certainly after the age of 30. There is usually a happy medium that will be right for you. Don't be afraid to experiment; one of the great advantages of hair is that it grows back (at the rate of about half an inch per month), so if you make a mistake, it will naturally correct itself within a relatively short space of time. Settle on a style and length that works best with your face and shows it off to advantage. This is one of the reasons adolescent boys are inclined to grow their hair long: it hides features to which they are still becoming accustomed. By adulthood, you ought to have worked out what are your best facial attributes, and decided on a hairstyle that complements them. Consider changing your hair as you grow older. The wild style you wore as a youth probably doesn't look so good now that your hair has turned gray. It is possible your choice of hair length and style will be governed by your career. Many jobs require employees to keep their hair short and neat. Sometimes, as with the military and police force, this is an official ruling. More often it is an informal but universally understood directive, especially in professions like banking or law. As with so much else about our appearance, there is no logic behind this, simply awareness that we are all judged, consciously or unconsciously, on the basis of how we look. Short, tidy hair is deemed to indicate reliability whereas, for the past century, long hair has been considered evidence of a rebellious temperament (not a quality prized in the military or in financial services), and therefore unacceptable. For this reason, longer hair tends to be found mainly among men working in more creative professions, such as advertising or broadcasting.

Taking care of your hair

Washing

Cleanliness is as important as tidiness. You need to wash your hair regularly, but just how often depends on a number of factors: how greasy it becomes over successive days, for example, and in what sort of environment you work and live. Another factor to be taken into account is the buildup of styling products in your hair, which have to be cleaned out after a few days. Nevertheless, bear in mind that too much washing is harmful, since it strips the scalp of naturally defensive oils and does not allow time for them to be replenished. Even if you only wash your hair twice a week, do so with a gentle shampoo and conditioner. Avoid any products with too many chemicals and perfumes, as these could cause an allergic reaction.

Dandruff

A common phenomenon among men is dandruff; seemingly, it affects half the post-pubertal population. Dandruff is residual evidence of the scalp shedding dead skin cells. In itself dandruff is not dirty or harmful, but it looks unattractive to have a blanket of white flakes on your shoulders and can be the cause of embarrassment. Most cases can be treated and resolved by using one of the anti-dandruff shampoos widely available. Again, be aware that some of the contents in your shampoo and conditioner, or in your styling products, may be exacerbating an inclination toward dandruff. Sometimes just changing one of these items results in a return to dandruff-free hair. If the problem is more extreme and defies home treatment, it will be necessary to see a dermatologist who will be able to prescribe an appropriate solution, such as the topical application of corticosteroids that combat skin conditions.

Styling products

After washing and drying your hair, you will most probably want to finish with one or more styling products. Until the 1980s, there used to be only one such item available to men, Brylcreem, a pomade invented in 1928 which left evidence of its presence in your hair on shirt collars, sheets and pillow cases, and any other fabric it touched. More recently, other options have become available and today, as even the most cursory glance over supermarket shelves will testify, there is a daunting range of styling products on offer.

Once more, the only way to discover what works best for

your hair is engaging in a process of trial and error. Aside from gels, there are many mousses, pastes, creams, and serums, the work of any or all of which can be finished off with a spritz or more of hairspray. The purpose of these products is to help your hair stay neat through the course of a day.

Accordingly, the perfect scenario should be that your hair remains in place but is not so locked into position that anyone wishing to run a hand through it encounters an impenetrable helmet. The popularity among the young for gravity-defying hairstyles, in particular great tufts of hair that shoot skyward from the forehead, should be the cause of amusement not emulation. This style is achieved only by the deployment of industrial quantities of hair gel and spray, and is so brittle it could probably be snapped off. Rest assured: any man who at present wears his hair in this way will, in a few years' time, be paying serious money to ensure all photographic evidence of his tonsorial misdemeanor is destroyed. Again, it is essential you don't betray the fact that time and effort went into your hair grooming; those locks must look as though they artfully arranged themselves on your scalp. Never overload your hair with styling product because, once again, this could cause an adverse reaction. In addition, too much product is harder to remove when you wash your hair, so apply the minimum necessary.

To dye or not to dye?

Should men color their hair? Not so many years ago, nobody would have thought to ask such a question; just as men never used anything in their hair except a dab of Brylcreem, so they lived and died with whatever color their hair was at the time

(as opposed to living and dying). Personal intervention in the matter was absolutely inconceivable. Not so today, when many men do color their hair, either choosing to visit a hairdresser for a professional application, or doing the job themselves with one of the kits available in many supermarkets, drugstores, and pharmacies.

Professional work on your hair will usually take the form of highlights and lowlights, that is, applying a hair colorant to strands of your hair. This can be done with the use of foil, with a brush, or by methods known as "frosting" and "clunking," which broadly involve a more free-hand approach to using dye. There is also the process of bleaching, which effectively strips the natural color from your hair. Home kits tend to feature a brush, although they can also allow for the application of a single color to your whole head. Incidentally, other than price there appears to be no real difference between the kits sold to men and those targeted at women (the former usually prove to be more expensive).

Ultimately, it is a matter of personal choice but once you engage in hair coloring it becomes difficult to stop. Like Botox or cosmetic surgery, dyeing hair requires ongoing—and potentially costly—maintenance, otherwise after a couple of weeks its presence will be apparent as your natural hair color begins to appear at the roots. Young men tend to dye their hair because it is fashionable. Older men, on the other hand, most often do so because they want to hide evidence that they are going gray. It is true that gray hair can make you appear older than you might wish, but so can many other things, such as drab skin or lack of animation in your features. In a competitive job market, youthfulness, with its accompanying attributes of energy and enthusiasm, is at a premium. So it is understandable that signs of aging can be unwelcome. Nevertheless, ultimately you will find engaging with hair dye a self-defeating process: there are few more visible signs of creeping age than hair that is unnaturally rich in color above a lined face. Better to leave your hair its natural color, even if this is gray or white, and find other means of projecting youthful dynamism.

Here is a brief guide to what hair style works best with each facial shape:

• **Oval Face:** Generally considered the ideal, since it is most balanced, and almost any hair style will suit. But other features, like your nose, might be more prominent than average, so take this into account when making your decision.

• **Long Face:** You want to diminish length, so opt for a hair style that is longer and fuller on the sides and relatively short on top, as this will help to provide balance.

• **Triangular Face:** Is wider at the forehead than the chin and often has prominent cheekbones. A long fringe or bangs, perhaps with a side parting, will help to even the impression (and a beard is also advantageous in filling out the lower section of the face).

- **Round Face:** You will want to lengthen your features, so no full or wide hair styles. Instead, go for the reverse of what is prescribed for men with long faces, i.e. keep the hair short at the sides and fuller on top.

- **Square Face:** Not dissimilar from the round face, but with a more defined jawline and sometimes skull. In this instance, still keep hair short at the sides and with a soft fullness on top of the head.

- **Diamond Face:** Widest in the middle around the cheekbones. To play down this feature, wear your hair longer at the sides and have a full fringe or bangs on top.

Losing your hair

And so to baldness, which again can be the cause of much angst. Hair loss usually begins on either side of the forehead, with the resultant receding hairline, and on the crown of the head. Eventually the two meet and you are undeniably and inescapably bald. Genetic inheritance is the most common reason for losing your hair: if other males in your family, either maternal or paternal, went bald, you're also likely to do so. Seemingly, DHT, a form of testosterone, is responsible for inducing baldness, so all those stories about bald men being more virile have at least some basis in truth. On the other hand, just to complicate matters, one of the main reasons why older men lose their hair is because there is a decrease in the amount of testosterone the body will produce. Whatever the explanation, the fact remains that if you're genetically predisposed to baldness, it will more than likely happen.

There are a number of responses you can have to this condition. One is denial, which usually involves growing whatever hair you still have and then tortuously wrapping or scraping it across your scalp to give the (not very convincing) impression that you still luxuriate in tonsorial splendor. You will dread strong winds lest they disturb your artwork and reveal the baldness beneath. For the same reason, you will also live in fear of anyone touching your hair.

Secondly, you can seek out treatment to restore or replace your missing hair. There are a huge number of options available today, ranging from oral applications to operations. Some are more successful than others; all are likely to cost you a lot of money. If, however, your baldness is costing you even more angst, then finding a means to give you back a full head of hair will be deemed a price worth paying. As with gray hair, it seems men worry that baldness makes them look prematurely old and therefore less attractive or dynamic. But, again like gray hair, there are many ways to project a zestful personality other than the presentation of a fully follicled scalp.

Another possibility is that you wear a wig. This used to be a more widespread recourse than is now the case. You can choose from wigs made of human hair, horsehair, or various synthetic materials. Realistically, you shouldn't consider any of them. Of all the options open to you, a wig is the least attractive.

Finally, you can accept that you're going or have gone bald, and not give the matter any further thought. This is without doubt the best course of action and the one that will cost you least, either in worry or money. If you are losing your hair, cut what remains short. Your barber can run a trimmer over your scalp and ensure an even appearance. There are also electrical devices you can buy to perform the same task at home. As with so much else about your appearance, the most important point is that you look clean and tidy.

Chapter 4

Teeth

A good smile ought to be among your most engaging features; it will certainly be one of the features that people notice first about you. However, the impression you make will not be positive if you have poor teeth (or if, owing to the bad state of your teeth, you keep your mouth permanently clamped shut).

———•———

What are teeth?

The human tooth is made from calcium, phosphorus, and other mineral salts; the resultant core is called dentine, while the outer visible layer is known as enamel. Teeth are basically composed of two parts: a root to anchor the tooth into the maxilla (upper jaw) or mandible (lower jaw), and a crown that is outside the gum. We have four different kinds of teeth, which help us to break down and consume edible matter: incisors for cutting off bites of food; cuspids, or canines, for tearing food; premolars to tear and crush food; and molars to grind food. This quartet allows us humans to be omnivores, in other words, to eat both meat and vegetables.

Like other mammals, we develop two sets of teeth, the first of which—known as baby teeth—usually begin to develop within four months of birth but are then gradually replaced by more permanent teeth. There are 32 of these: six maxillary and six mandibular molars, four maxillary and four mandibular premolars, two maxillary and two mandibular canines, four maxillary and four mandibular incisors. The molars at the very back of the mouth, upper and lower, are the final teeth to appear, usually in your late teens/early twenties, and hence these are known as wisdom teeth. Because they only arrive after the others, they can become "impacted," that is to come in sideways with consequences for the teeth already in place. For this reason they are often removed.

The impression you make on prospective partners will not be positive if you have poor teeth

While not as unique to an individual as fingerprints, teeth can be invaluable in establishing a person's identity and are therefore the subject of study by forensic dentists. A number of criminal trials in which convictions were secured thanks to dental evidence established the soundness of forensic odontology. In 1948, for example, English pathologist Keith Simpson used bite marks on the breast of the victim to ensure Robert Gorringe was convicted for the murder of his wife Phyllis. Similarly in California in 1975, Walter Marx was convicted of sexual assault and murder after bite marks on the victim's nose were compared with dental impressions given by the suspect and found to be the same. In other words, if you intend to commit a crime, make sure your teeth aren't involved.

An oral history

Despite all the work they have to do, and all the neglect they frequently suffer, our teeth are remarkably resilient. Long after much of the rest of our corpse has disintegrated, teeth continue to survive. For this reason, their recovery from preserved skeletal remains is an essential part of ancient DNA and archaeological research. When bodies are discovered by archaeologists, any remaining teeth will be carefully analyzed to provide data about the person's age, eating habits, and lifestyle. One of the reasons we now know so much about prehistoric man is through the examination of his teeth. Long after you are dead, and provided your remains have not been cremated, it will be possible for subsequent generations to learn how you lived and what you ate by studying your teeth.

Accordingly, if you want to make a good impression, not just today but for centuries to come, you should start looking after the contents of your mouth. Many people believe this process inevitably involves a visit to the dentist. Of course, it is possible and sometimes necessary to spend large sums of money on dental work, with the end result being a perfect set of upper and lower teeth. However, a basic daily care routine will help to minimize trips to the dentist and drive down costs when you do so.

If you want to make a good impression, you should start looking after the contents of your mouth

Brushing your teeth thoroughly every morning and evening is the prerequisite. By doing so, you will remove dental plaque and tartar, thereby preventing the development of cavities, gingivitis, and gum disease: the last of these apparently causes at least a third of all adult tooth loss. Plaque is a biofilm, usually pale yellow, formed by colonizing bacteria attaching themselves to the surface of the tooth. You must not allow this colonization to occur, otherwise decay is liable to follow. Tooth decay is a global problem, due to food being left inside pits and fissures on chewing surfaces. The way to avoid this happening to you is by making sure you clean your teeth regularly.

There is a long history of devices created for the purpose: in ancient times, twigs, bird quills, and even animal bones were used. However, the modern bristle toothbrush seems to have been invented in China. One account from the early 13th century mentions monks cleaning their teeth with brushes of ox-bone handle into which horse-tail hairs had been fitted. Travelers to Asia brought such devices back to Europe where they began to become widespread during the 17th century. Prior to that period, teeth were commonly cleaned with either a chewing stick (basically a twig that had been chewed to create a splayed end) or a rag. In both cases, an abrasive like coal dust or salt would be applied to the surface and then rubbed onto the teeth: not, we can agree, the most effective or pleasant form of cleaning.

The first mass-produced toothbrush is credited to Londoner William Addis, a rag-trader who, having been jailed in 1780 for causing a riot (objecting, perhaps, to the state of the nation's dental hygiene?) used his time in prison to devise an implement for cleaning teeth. According to legend, this consisted of a bone left over from a meal he had earlier enjoyed and through which he drilled a number of holes, filling these with tufts of bristle provided by a friendly guard, and sealed into place with glue. On emerging from incarceration, Addis started to produce his toothbrushes commercially and the business blossomed, continuing to this day, although now known as Wisdom. By the 19th century, toothbrushes were being mass-produced throughout Europe and the United States, and their use had become commonplace. The big changes that have since occurred concern the materials used in their manufacture. Animal bristle, not ideal because it is inclined to retain bacteria, was replaced by synthetic fibers, most often nylon, and the handle likewise is no longer made from a natural material but a form of thermoplastic. The first commercial electric toothbrush, called the Broxodent, was invented in Switzerland in 1954 and subsequent similar devices soon became hugely popular.

According to independent research, electric toothbrushes are no more effective than their manual equivalent—provided they are used properly. What matters most is not the tool but the way it is employed: you can brush your teeth just as badly with an electric as with a manual toothbrush.

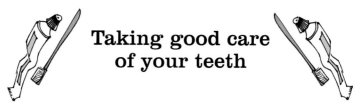

Taking good care of your teeth

So how should you be brushing? Well, first of all the process should take at least two minutes and cover back as well as front teeth. Make sure you don't miss out on any areas. Start with the outer surfaces, working from the back forward. Try to spend some time on the inside of your teeth before finishing, paying extra attention to the biting surfaces. Always brush from gum to tooth and do not use a jerking vertical motion, as this can lead to gum recession and the exposure of parts of your teeth not protected by enamel.

Toothpaste

In this task, you are likely to use toothpaste. Like toothbrushes, this has a long and sometimes equally unattractive history (soot and salt have already been mentioned). The main function of tooth cleaning materials in the past was to provide an element of abrasion in order to remove traces of food. So the ancient Greeks and Romans used crushed bones or oyster shells, which sound only marginally more appealing than coal dust. Until the end of the 19th century, tooth powders were the norm, rather than pastes, and they could be made from a diverse range of ingredients, to which water would be added. Pastes were gradually introduced from the 1890s onward, with various flavors added to make them more palatable (and to give the user that "fresh breath" experience). Fluoride, which can help to prevent dental decay, was introduced around the same time as pastes made their debut, but only became widespread from the 1950s onward.

Modern toothpastes perform much the same function as their ancient equivalents, albeit in a more attractive fashion. Mostly they provide abrasion, together with a pleasant aftertaste. Any additional claims should be regarded with a degree of skepticism. The ability of toothpastes to clean, and to whiten, is limited: the most important aspect to looking after your teeth lies in good brushing technique, not in the ingredients of your paste. A small but important point: change your toothbrush regularly, at least once every three months. Otherwise the bristles become too worn and can no longer do their job effectively. And rinse the brush head in very hot water after every use, to minimize the risk of germs collecting and causing infection in your mouth.

Flossing

Don't imagine that once you have finished brushing your teeth, all maintenance work is done. Next you should floss. Dental floss is made from a series of micro-fine filaments, which are gently inserted between two teeth and then scraped along their respective surfaces in order to remove any residue of food or plaque. A New Orleans dentist called Levi Spear Parmly apparently proposed floss, made from silk fibers, in 1815 but the call was largely ignored; only at the very end of the 19th century did Johnson & Johnson take out the first commercial patent for dental floss. Take-up remained poor, however, until around the time of World War II, when nylon floss was invented and proved to be better than silk, having greater abrasion resistance and elasticity.

Despite the widely appreciated benefits of flossing, many people continue only to brush their teeth. For the sake of your dental hygiene, you should do both, and should learn how to floss properly. Wind a piece of the filament approximately 18 inches long between the middle fingers of your two hands. Next, gently but firmly slide a piece of floss up and down between each pair of teeth, making sure you reach under the gum line. Move the floss along between your fingers so that you are not using the same strip between all teeth. If you are not used to flossing, you may find your gums bleed—don't let this put you off. Bleeding is just a temporary reaction and your gums will grow healthier and stronger thanks to a regular flossing routine.

The interdental brush

Follow with a third piece of equipment: the interdental brush. This is a small device with disposable heads fitted onto a plastic handle that is deployed to remove any remaining bits of food trapped between teeth. It is also invaluable for cleaning between the wire of dental braces, if you are wearing these. Interdental brushes come in a variety of sizes and you will need to find which one is right for you, depending on the width of gaps between teeth. As with toothbrushes, change your interdental brush on a routine basis.

Mouthwash

And now, it is time to conclude with a rinse of mouthwash, although preferably with something better tasting than what was proposed by Hippocrates: the ancient Greek physician recommended an interesting mixture of salt, aluminum sulfate, and vinegar. Regardless of any claims made on the container in relation to whitening or bacteria-killing, do not expect too much from your mouthwash. It is not a substitute for any of the previous activities but complements and concludes them, leaving you with a clean mouth and fresh breath. Many dentists recommend using a mouthwash low in, or free of, alcohol.

The dentist

Speaking of dentists, you ought to schedule an appointment every six months or so, in order to have your teeth checked. If you have been taking good care of them and following the twice-daily regime outlined above, the dentist will have little to do other than congratulate you on your admirable oral hygiene. But there may be problems lurking beneath the surface that only a dentist can detect (taking x-rays is now a standard procedure) and, as in all other areas of medicine, prevention is superior to cure, as well as usually being the cheaper option.

In any case, your visit will also provide an opportunity to have your teeth examined by a dental hygienist who can assess your current regime and perhaps encourage better practice: it is surprising how many of us don't even brush our teeth properly, let alone follow through with adequate flossing and interdental cleaning. Learning good oral health is invaluable because it will lead to less work being performed on your teeth (with consequent cost savings).

The other advantage to scheduling regular dental surgery visits is that they should include a professional cleaning of your teeth. Bear in mind that some food and drink you take in your mouth is likely to discolor teeth. Villains include tea, coffee, and red wine; the more you consume of these, the more likely there is to be evidence of their intake on your teeth. Cigarette smoking is also harmful to your teeth: nicotine not only builds up stains but also inflicts damage on the enamel and gums. Even with the most rigorous efforts on your part, it is probable that tartar, which is mineralized plaque, will have built up in those parts of your mouth that are hardest to reach with a toothbrush and dental floss. Professional cleaning ensures this is cleared away, that your teeth are given a good polish, and all evidence of what you have been consuming in recent months is removed.

Whiter than white

Do you want, or need, to go further? There are a number of procedures offered by dentists that will improve, or even fundamentally alter, the appearance of your teeth. The most common of these is whitening. It is a fact that as we age, the mineral content of our teeth changes due to enamel becoming less porous and more mineral-deficient. In other words, yellow teeth in the elderly are not necessarily a sign of dental decay. But since white teeth are highly prized, all of us would prefer to keep the contents of our mouth that color.

You can now buy teeth-whitening kits for use at home. These work by the application of a bleaching agent, usually placed in a plastic tray, which is then fitted onto the upper and lower jaw for a short period. There are also mouthguards and dental strips that perform the same function, although the latter will contain a lower concentration of bleaching agent and therefore produce weaker results. The effectiveness of these whiteners varies widely from one individual to the next.

In addition, each jurisdiction's health authority tends to permit different levels of bleaching agent; in some countries, it is very low and likely to have a negligible impact on the color of your teeth.

There are obvious advantages to having your teeth whitened by a professional, not least the assurance that the procedure will yield visible results. Furthermore, before any whitening takes place, your teeth ought to be scrupulously examined in advance to make sure the process will not lead to any side-effects. A good dentist will curb your wish to have excessively white teeth. Naturally, if you are spending money on whitening, which is never cheap, you will want the best possible outcome. But bear in mind that teeth that appear too white, like teeth that are uniformly even, will not look natural, especially if you are no longer in the first flush of youth. The most efficacious intervention should be the least apparent. Far from improving your appearance in an undetectable fashion, dazzling white teeth will clearly proclaim that work has been done on your mouth. Resist the temptation to go for snow-white teeth and settle on a lighter shade than is presently the case but still one that is credible for a man of your age.

The same rule applies to any other dental procedure you undertake: there should be no evidence it ever occurred. Sometimes work is essential—such as having a crown or an implant—sometimes optional, like having old metal fillings replaced with white ones. More adults today than used to be the case consider having their teeth straightened, which involves wearing braces for several months or even longer. There are various kinds of braces, including a clear variety

for anyone who feels self-conscious about the process. You could be wearing braces for cosmetic reasons or because your dentist feels it necessary to correct a problem like a defective under- or overbite. Whatever the reason, make sure the outcome leaves the contents of your mouth looking better than they did before, but not looking unnaturally flawless. It is the small imperfections in our features, such as a gap between two front teeth, which render us distinctive from everyone else. Homogeneity, even in matters dental, is not to be encouraged.

Chapter 5

Body, Hands,
and Feet

John Wesley, the 18th-century founder of
Methodism, once famously declared that
cleanliness is indeed next to godliness.
Consequently, your chances of becoming a
living deity will be immeasurably improved
if you are able to maintain a continual state
of cleanliness. Failure to do so will not only
diminish your godlike status but also find
you shunned by the majority of the
population—particularly by members of the
opposite sex or anyone in close proximity
to you—as an accumulation of body odor
renders your company steadily more
offensive. Just as our clothes need to be
washed regularly to keep them clean, so,
too, do our bodies.

Body

Failure to wash leads to poor hygiene, which, in turn, renders us more vulnerable to disease and infection. One of the most important ways in which Florence Nightingale improved standards of nursing in Victorian Britain was to insist on basic hygiene in hospitals. As a result, levels of infection and mortality among patients dropped.

Cleanliness is indispensable to our modern notion of social perfection

Bodily cleanliness is regularly equated with moral purity: clean people are deemed to be good people. The Christian faith, for example, proposes the notion that sins are washed away in the sacrament of baptism, which is a form of ritual cleansing. Likewise, Muslims consider it important that believers should be clean in body and spirit alike, with Mohammed declaring, "A Muslim is required to be pure morally and spiritually as well as physically." This link between cleanliness and goodness means dirt is often proclaimed as "bad," although it has no inherent behavioral characteristics. All of which helps to explain why Wesley ascribed godliness to the clean.

"Cleanliness," wrote the 19th-century cultural historian Jacob Burckhardt, "is indispensable to our modern notion of social perfection." When he made this statement over 150 years ago, general standards of cleanliness and opportunities to become and remain clean were far less widespread than is the case today. Improvements in plumbing since 1900 mean we are much cleaner than our ancestors, for whom bathing was an infrequent activity, performed perhaps once a week at most. While the ancient Romans had large public baths that were open to, and frequented by, all citizens, thereafter access to such facilities greatly declined, with a corresponding drop in standards of cleanliness. Even the act of assembling and heating sufficient water for a bath meant few people troubled to wash themselves much. As a result, the past was not only another country, to quote L.P. Hartley's dictum, but also a much smellier one.

There is no longer any reason for you to remain unwashed unless you are making some kind of personal protest against the act of bathing, or decline to clean yourself on obscure ethical grounds. Although too much washing can lead to dry and rough skin—water strips our bodies of their natural oils—we ought to bathe once a day. Whether you take a bath or shower is a matter of personal choice, but it should be pointed out that baths use up more water and are therefore more expensive, as well as time-consuming. There is also an argument to be made that when you sit in a bath, you are effectively wallowing in your own dirt. While an occasional bath can be recommended, especially as a means of relieving sore muscles after extreme exertion or to ease tension at the end of a stressful day, this should probably not be your customary means of washing.

In a world where water is an increasingly precious and costly resource, showers are the best way to wash. They are fast and economical, and do the job just as well as—if not better than—a bath. When in the shower, the most important body parts to be cleansed on a daily basis are your armpits and groin area, both of which hold large concentrations of the apocrine sweat glands that first become active during puberty. We need to sweat or, to use the more genteel term, perspire, because this is our body's form of thermoregulation. As we become too warm, our skin yields moisture, the evaporation of which has a cooling effect. So we sweat in order to cool down. On average, men perspire more quickly than women and produce greater quantities of sweat, particularly when engaged in exercise.

Dealing with excess perspiration

Some men sweat more than others, and if you are a heavy sweater, this can be embarrassing, especially in today's Western culture where it is deemed ideal to remain perspiration-free at all times: keeping your cool means remaining devoid of sweat. At his party conference in 2000, Britain's then-Prime Minister Tony Blair was photographed delivering a speech in a blue shirt drenched in sweat, and while efforts were made to proclaim this a sign of his passion, it is notable that politicians ever since have studiously avoided wearing colored shirts at key moments in their careers. So opposed is our society to visible evidence of perspiration that, of late, there has been a fashion for underarm Botox injections: just as the toxin can freeze the muscles on your forehead and stop you frowning, so it paralyzes the nerve endings of sweat glands.

There is a condition called hyperhidrosis, otherwise known as excessive sweating. All of us have suffered from this at some time or another, usually when we find ourselves in the middle of a heatwave or a situation that leaves us feeling uncomfortable. But for some men this is a serious issue caused by over-active sweat glands and can be treated either by medication or, in certain circumstances, by surgery (which results in removal of the glands).

We all have a unique scent, one that is detectable to everyone both physically and emotionally close to us

Obviously there is nothing inherently dirty about sweat: it is simply a mechanical process that we share with many other mammals. While perspiration is composed primarily of water, it also contains small quantities of minerals, lactic acid, and urea. If this combination of elements remains on our skin for too long, particularly in zones like the underarm area where little light or air penetrates, they will start to ferment and produce what can, over time, become an unpleasant smell. This is why we need to wash ourselves, in anticipation of developing body odor, more usually known as BO. Wash the regions where this is most prevalent with a soap-free cleanser and afterward rinse thoroughly.

As for the rest of your body, unless particular areas are especially dirty, you need be less scrupulous. Bear in mind that we all have a unique scent, one that is detectable to everyone both physically and emotionally close to us. You don't want to lose one of the traits specific to you by over-assiduous scrubbing or, indeed, the excessive use of perfume (of which more later); that would be like destroying part of your DNA.

After drying yourself thoroughly with a clean towel, you will most likely want to apply a deodorant or antiperspirant. It's worth pointing out the differences between the two products since they are often considered to perform the same task. Deodorants do not interfere with the production of sweat but prevent the development of odor through the presence of antiseptic agents, and very often by the addition of a fragrance. The first commercial deodorant was invented around the end of the 19th century and marketed as Mum. Antiperspirants, on the other  hand, only became available in the 1940s. Unlike deodorants, these products contain chemical compounds that are designed to block your pores to inhibit the discharge of sweat. As a rule, they are also scented. Antiperspirants contain aluminum compounds as an active ingredient to stop sweat forming. A small number of people will be allergic to this ingredient and develop a skin rash but for most of us there are no side effects. You could find yourself suffering from skin burn due to excessive use of antiperspirant, so don't overdo it: sweating is a natural process intended to lower your body temperature and ought to be permitted, especially if you wash yourself often.

Should you sweat a lot, don't overlook the merits of talcum powder, a natural mineral composed of magnesium silicate. Today it is mostly used on babies to prevent the development of nappy rash, but the powder's absorbent qualities make it a useful ally in countering evidence of perspiration. After you have washed and dried yourself, rub some talc over your body and you'll find it helps to keep you dry over the coming hours.

Your hands

Hands are one of the most hardworking parts of our body, yet we are inclined to take them for granted and show little appreciation of their sterling efforts. They are also one of the first things, along with good teeth and clear eyes, that other people will notice about us. For this reason it is important that we put the best hand forward whenever in company, yet it is astonishing how many men fail to do so. Instead, they frequently present a pair of paws that are calloused and covered in cuts, with ragged, untidy nails, each loaded with a generous quantity of dirt.

No doubt, a lot of men mistakenly hold the opinion that paying attention to their hands is effeminate and/or a waste of their valuable time and money. Especially if they're employed in farming or construction work, their hands are likely to be subjected to a lot of abuse and, they would probably argue, the last thing they need to do is pamper their mitts with various lotions, creams, and treatments. Well, perhaps they should think a little less about themselves and a little more about the rest of us, particularly their partners and families, who have to put up with their hoary hands on a regular basis.

Failure to look after your hands can be regarded as due to nothing better than foolish indifference

They might also like to take into account that a small amount of care could have the effect of ensuring they do an even better job than is now the case: coarse and rough hands lose their sensitivity, making them less capable than those that have been well maintained of performing tasks that require a certain level of dexterity. In any case, and especially in contemporary urban environments, the majority of men are not professionally engaged in activities that demand their hands are submitted to regular misuse. Since when was tapping a computer keyboard or clicking the button on a mouse so physically demanding on our hands? Ought holding a cell phone and sending a text message be deemed manual labor? Under these circumstances, failure to look after your hands can be regarded as due to nothing better than foolish indifference and laziness.

Basic hand care

The first, and most obvious, task is to keep your hands clean. This means washing them regularly (and, one might add here, especially after visiting the lavatory; it is truly astonishing how many men seem to believe they needn't engage in this elementary act of social courtesy). There is a much wider appreciation today than was formerly the case of how infectious bacilli and viral infections are spread through unwashed hands. In recent years, the importance of clean hands has become particularly important in hospitals, where various potentially life-threatening illnesses can be caught simply because someone in the building did not engage in

this basic act. A 2009 report into the subject by the Scottish National Health Service noted that, "Hand hygiene is considered to be the single most important way to stop the spread of germs. If the hands of those caring for a patient, as well as the hands of the patient and their family/visitors, are kept clean, then the risk of the patient getting an infection will be far less." Similarly, in the United States it has been estimated that in the region of 100,000 people die annually from hospital-acquired infections. Many of these deaths could be prevented were more medical workers to keep their hands well washed and sanitized throughout the day. So even if you're not a doctor or nurse, you have an obligation to the rest of us to wash your hands thoroughly and regularly.

Dirty, unkempt nails will reflect badly on you and cannot be tolerated

Rough and calloused hands are not pleasant either to look at or to feel. They will let you down, particularly if you have taken trouble over the rest of your appearance. Keep the skin on your hands soft by investing in a tube of hand cream and make a point of applying it every day. If, during the winter, you suffer from chilblains, a condition caused by cold and humidity, and leading to redness, itching, and cracked skin, make sure to apply plenty of strong hand cream to counter the complaint. One way to ensure less pain is to wear cotton gloves in bed at night, putting them on after you have coated your hands in cream: while you sleep, this is absorbed into the skin. White cotton gloves in a variety of sizes can be bought in any pharmacy.

Dirty, unkempt nails will reflect badly on you and cannot be tolerated. If you watch black and white films from the 1930s and 1940s, you will frequently see the protagonist receiving a professional manicure. This procedure has now fallen from favor among men but it is perfectly possible for you to perform the same job in your own home. An undemanding and simple procedure, it takes just a few minutes and can be done while you're sitting in front of the television. Begin by keeping the surface beneath your nails clean, using a brush designed for this purpose while you are taking a bath or shower. The shaped end of a nail file will allow you to remove any excess dirt. Gently nudge it between nail and skin without pushing too hard against the latter.

Using either scissors or clippers, trim your nails at least once a week so that they are never more than about one-eighth of an inch in length. Tidy off each nail edge by running an emery board along the top to leave a consistent smooth curve. Nail-biting is a childish habit for which there is no excuse in adulthood. Not only will it make you look puerile but your hands will also look a mess.

Your feet

At least during the winter months, your feet will most likely not be as visible as your hands, but that doesn't mean they're undeserving of the same care. In fact, since more men wear sandals for more of the time each year, it becomes imperative that they take care of their feet, if only to spare the rest of us the sight of their hoary gnarled toes and heels. Should you be one of those individuals who believe flip-flops represent the future of footwear, then give a thought for everyone else and put only your best foot forward.

In addition, your feet are entitled to a little TLC, not least as a reward for the literal support they give you every day: those two little protrusions at the bottom of your legs keep you upright and allow you to move forward in the world. Give them the credit and the attention they deserve.

Establishing a routine

You will find that a once-weekly foot care regime will help to minimize odor and avoid the build up of cracked or scaly skin and calluses. Take time one evening out of seven to soak your feet in warm water into which a little cider vinegar has been added. After a couple of minutes of soaking remove all areas of callusing, especially on the heel and around the top of your toes, with a pumice stone or exfoliating metal scrub, either of which can be bought in any decent pharmacy. Next, cut and tidy up your toenails, rounding them off with a little file. After drying your feet, apply a moisturizing cream similar to that

used on your hands; this will minimize the build-up of calluses over the next week.

Keeping your feet in good condition will help to minimize the likelihood of unpleasant smells. Foot odor derives from the build-up of sweat because this is one of those parts of our anatomy prone to moisture outbreaks. As with sweat elsewhere, the condition isn't inherently smelly but becomes so if left untreated. This is especially the case if you wear the same shoes every day and don't allow them to rest between use: remember, shoes usually have poor ventilation, so bad smells are liable to become trapped. Socks made from artificial fibers like polyester and nylon generally also provide less ventilation and may encourage more perspiration than those manufactured from cotton or wool. Only buy the latter and change them, along with your shoes, on a daily basis. If you suffer from a severe dose of foot odor, it can be rectified by the deployment of sodium bicarbonate, an ingredient that is also used in baking. Rub a few pinches of this onto the soles of your feet every day, and put a few inside your shoes as well, and you will find the bad smells soon disappear. There are many commercial products available, usually insoles for shoes, which are designed to do the same job, but sodium bicarbonate is cheaper and just as effective.

And always remember that the quality of shoes you wear will have a direct effect on the state of your feet. Ill-fitting and poor-quality footwear should be avoided, as should be wearing the same shoes on consecutive days. Keep your feet in top condition and you will be the principal beneficiary.

Chapter 6

Bodily Adornment

Early human societies were much given to bodily adornment, most likely owing to a shortage of good tailors. Unable to order a decent suit, one sufficiently well-cut to disguise his thickening waistline and sloping shoulders, primitive man resorted to other distractions, such as a bone belonging to a deceased enemy worn through his septum. Thankfully, over the intervening millennia we have grown more sophisticated in our presentation, and less inclined to wear parts of our opponents.

Tattoos

The practice of tattooing dates back to the Neolithic period. The word, however, is a relatively recent addition to the English language, courtesy of the naturalist and botanist Sir Joseph Banks, who accompanied Captain James Cook on his voyage around the world on board HMS *Endeavour* (1768–1771). In his journal for August 1769, Banks, who was then in Tahiti, wrote in his logbook of the indigenous population: "I shall now mention their method of painting their bodies, or 'tattow,' as it is called in their language. This they do by inlaying the color black under their skins in such a manner as to be indelible; everyone is marked thus in different parts of his body accordingly maybe to his humor or different circumstances of his life."

Tattooing is a more ancient and widespread form of body adornment than was then realized by Banks. In 1991, the body of a man who had died some 5,200 years ago was discovered on the Austro-Italian border in the Alps. On his body were some 58 tattoos—simple dots and little crosses distributed in a seemingly random manner. However, further investigation suggested that the tattoos' location—on the lower spine and at knee and ankle joints—indicated they were applied in the hope of alleviating pain, likely caused by arthritis, and accordingly intended to be therapeutic rather than a mark of social status.

On the other hand, the latter function has often been the reason for the application of tattoos. In pre-Christian Britain, for example, tattooing among tribal leaders was widespread. In fact, one tribe living in eastern and northern Scotland, the Picts, are so named because the Romans knew them as "Picti," that is, "painted people."

The Romans themselves did not engage in tattooing, except for criminals and slaves, in other words as a means of demonstrating the lowest status: a legal inscription found in Ephesus indicates that slaves exported to Asia were tattooed with the words "tax paid." Soldiers and gladiators also took to having their faces tattooed but this practice was banned in the 4th century by the Emperor Constantine after he converted to Christianity, since he believed it disfigured "that made in God's image."

It is astonishing to see how, more than 1,700 years after this imperial prohibition, tattooing has returned to widespread fashion. Various arguments have been made to present the practice as perfectly acceptable, not least on the basis of historical precedent. However, do not presume that antiquity ensures respectability (note that in ancient times it was mostly slaves or soldiers who were tattooed), or that just because certain people in positions of authority once wore tattoos you are now justified in doing so. For example, it is often noted that George V had a dragon tattooed on one of his arms in 1882 while in Japan, and Queen Victoria was rumored to have a small tattoo on her person. That was then, this is now. Besides, since when did the British royal family start acting as the measure for correct behavior? Henry VIII had six wives, two of whom he executed: would you cite him as a role model in any discussion on marriage? It is also worth pointing out that at the time he acquired the aforementioned tattoo, George V was a teenager serving in the Royal Navy and not expected to become King (his older brother was then still alive). The combination of these circumstances and, in particular, the fact that he was an adolescent and really ought to have asked his parents' permission first, absolves him from responsibility for his actions. And unless you are likewise a royal teen visiting the Far East, it also absolves you from any obligation to imitate George V's behavior. The other role model in this area is David Beckham. Again, unless you are a multimillionaire soccer player with an underwear-advertising contract and your own range of sportswear, there is no need for you to have one or several tattoos.

Unless you plan to flash your Mensa membership card alongside your tattoos, you can expect 25 percent of people you encounter to assume you are dim

Tattoos frequently seem to be acquired when the wearer is drunk and/or under the influence of other substances. This information is based on one viewing of *The Hangover Part II* while on a long-haul flight, but that does not necessarily invalidate its merit. After all, if, like the unfortunate character in that film, you had a chance to evaluate the advantages of acquiring a tattoo in the chill light of day, it is probable you would decide against doing so, not least because of societal judgment. A survey carried out in the United States in

January 2012 found that while one in five adults now has a tattoo, two in five of the people questioned thought tattoo wearers were less attractive, and more than a quarter of them believed tattoo wearers were less intelligent than the rest of society. This judgment is irrational and unfair, but unless you plan to flash your Mensa membership card alongside your tattoos, you can expect over 25 percent of the people you encounter to assume you are dim.

Tattoos are not indelible and can be removed, most commonly with laser treatment. However, this requires a series of visits to the relevant clinic, may leave scarring, and is much more expensive than the original cost of the tattoo. If you yearn to look rebellious (as, rather sweetly, did a quarter of those with tattoos in the 2012 survey), why not opt for the temporary effect achieved by an ink transfer? Then you can imagine yourself as an edgy rule-breaker over the course of a weekend before reverting to societal norms on Monday morning. And nobody will question your level of intelligence. It can be asserted without contradiction that gentlemen do not have tattoos.

Piercings

Gentlemen are not pierced in any place. There was a fashion in late Renaissance courts for men to wear one earring, from which would hang something precious like a large baroque pearl. In 1577 the Anglican clergyman William Harrison published his *Description of England* in which he commented, "Some lusty courtiers and gentlemen of courage do wear either rings of gold, stones, or pearls in their ears." Like all fads, this one soon passed and men reverted to leaving their earlobes unpierced.

Earlobes are deemed to be erogenous zones, areas of our body especially sensitive to pleasure, and this helps to explain the popularity of earrings

Piercing shares with tattoos both an ancient history and a popularity among primitive societies. The well-preserved mummy found on the Austro-Italian border in 1991 was not only heavily tattooed, he also had pierced ears. The world's oldest earrings, dating back to 2500 BC were found in a grave in the Sumerian city of Ur, once home to Abraham. And there are several Biblical references to earrings: during the Jewish exodus from Egypt, Aaron made a golden calf from melted earrings while Moses was otherwise preoccupied receiving the Ten Commandments on Mount Sinai.

It is not clear why people started to pierce their ears, although there seems to be consensus among historians that the practice had less to do with bodily adornment than with superstition: believing that demons could enter the body through ears, metal jewelry was placed in close proximity to ward them away. Later, sailors started to pierce their ears for various reasons: if they drowned, a gold earring would provide funds for a funeral; an earring was a symbol that the wearer had traveled around the world; a pierced ear improved vision (although quite how is never explained).

Both male and female members of many tribes in Africa and Asia engage in ear piercing, although this does not customarily involve a tidy pair of pearl studs. Sometimes it can be a form of conspicuous consumption: the more piercings you have and the larger amount of costly metal, the greater your wealth. Certain tribes use piercing as a mark of transition from childhood to adolescence. Others don't just make a tiny hole but stretch the lobe to allow for the insertion of ear plugs.

If you have multiple piercings, you were most likely christened with a name like Jonathan, but now prefer to be known as Crusty, and participate in protests against global banking

If you are planning to move to a remote district of Borneo or perhaps the outer reaches of the Amazonian jungle, then these activities will be of interest and you will want to conform to societal norms that also include living in a hut and catching your own food. If, however, you have settled on Western norms, then having your ear pierced may not be such a good idea. While the practice has become more commonplace among men since the 1960s, it is still considered somewhat alternative and more frequently found among the young: there are few more regrettable sights than a middle-aged man sporting an earring. Rebellion is something best left to youth, especially when it takes the form of a pierced earlobe.

Earlobes are deemed to be erogenous zones, areas of our body especially sensitive to pleasure, and this helps to explain the popularity of earrings, since they draw the observer's attention. While women traditionally wear a pair of earrings, the preference among men has often been for just one. This is probably less a matter of aesthetics than a concern among insecure males that they should not be confused with the opposite sex. But among gentlemen, the preference remains for none at all. There are plenty of ways to ensure you receive attention without puncturing your ears.

Likewise the rest of your face. Since the advent of punk in the late 1970s, there has been a small sub-culture reveling in multiple piercings. So eyebrow, nostril and septum, lip, tongue, labret (the area between lower lip and chin) are all deemed ripe for a ring or stud, examples of which can be found among the more endangered tribes of Central Africa. If you do this to yourself, you were most likely christened with a name like Jonathan, but now prefer to be known as Crusty, live in a commune, follow a strict vegan diet, roll your own cigarettes, keep a mongrel dog attached to a piece of rope, and participate in countless protests against global banking. You are also most likely to have several other, more serious, grooming issues that ought to be dealt with posthaste.

It is, of course, perfectly possible to pierce any part of the human anatomy, and some people have done so. Unlike facial piercings, these marks are not immediately apparent, provided the person with them remains dressed. Only when clothes are removed do body piercings make an appearance, usually an unexpected one. As a rule, these adornments are associated with erogenous zones like the nipple, navel, and genitals, with the purpose of increasing sexual stimulation. A gentleman will not have such piercings, but should you encounter them in someone else, just make sure good hygiene has been followed. Given their location, piercings of this character need to be kept clean at all times.

Manscaping

There is a chance that you are unfamiliar with the word manscaping. If so, you are also likely to be unfamiliar with the practice of male depilation, otherwise known as the removal of body hair. This is a relatively modern phenomenon but one that appears to have widespread appeal, especially among younger members of society. A survey in August 2012 by Britain's *FHM* magazine found that 64 percent of its readership manscaped regularly and only 12 percent admitted to never doing so.

Various explanations are proffered to explain the emergence of depilation among men. Among the most likely is that for those who regularly frequent a gym and seek to develop their body shape, hair removal allows muscle form to be more clearly defined: notice how all body builders are hairless, at least whenever they are competing. In addition, pornographic actors—both male and female—tend to remove all or most of their body hair, again to give more prominence to the attributes that have brought them notice. It has been posited that with the advent of the internet and more widespread access to pornographic material, a greater number of people have judged body hairlessness as something to emulate. So, according to this theory, women started to remove all or most of their pubic hair because they had seen this trend among performers in adult films. Total hair removal, or what might be described as a carefully sculpted remnant, is thought to look tidier and, in many people's minds, to be cleaner. Therefore, women have encouraged men to follow their example and remove most or all pubic hair for the same reasons.

Initially, manscaping was the preserve of that widely discussed but rarely sighted character, the metrosexual male—someone who was essentially urban in temperament and preoccupied with personal appearance.

An entirely hairless man can look not unlike a freshly plucked chicken: so if you do plan to engage in manscaping, leave at least some evidence of your former hirsuteness

A frequently cited metrosexual role model is the previously mentioned David Beckham, whose bodily hairlessness (and fondness for tattoos) have been much copied.

So manscaping has moved beyond the world of porn and, as the *FHM* statistic demonstrates, gone mainstream. In April 2012, the *New York Times* reported that around 70 percent of one Manhattan salon's business involved male bikini waxing. How far you want to go with this is a matter of personal preference, as well as a reflection of your age and location: it is more likely manscaped bodies will be found among the young in large cities than among older country dwellers. Also variable are the means you use to remove your body hair. You can find electrical razors and trimmers for sale which allow the job to be done in the privacy of your own home. Alternatively, any urban center staking a claim to sophistication will have a salon capable of providing such a service to men using treatments already familiar to women, such as waxing. This requires wax to be applied to the body in strips, which are then pulled off, taking with them all the attached hair; the process is painful but effective. There are creams available that do much the same thing with less discomfort, and there is even the possibility of permanent hair removal through electrolysis.

An entirely hairless man can look not unlike a freshly plucked chicken: scarcely the most enticing spectacle. So if you do plan to engage in manscaping, leave at least some evidence of your former hirsuteness. Think of the process as being similar to tidying up a garden; you want to keep the shrubbery neat rather than strip it bare. The only part of your anatomy that ought to be completely clear of hair is the back, which frequently sprouts growth from middle age onward. Remove every last follicle on your back, especially if you are planning to take off your clothes in public.

Chapter 7

Scents and Cosmetics

It's fascinating to see the various reasons advanced as to why humans wear perfume and have done so for thousands of years. Explanations fall into three broad categories, the first and most obvious being that scents hide other, less pleasant smells. There can be no doubt this was once a powerful argument in their favor but it holds less sway in our own age.

————•————

Scent

It is proposed that far from masking our natural scent, perfumes heighten or fortify them as a way of sending out signals of attractiveness to other people. According to this theory, perfume acts as a magnet, although anyone who has ever stood next to somebody drenched in an unpleasantly powerful fragrance (there were a lot of them manufactured in the 1980s) will argue otherwise. It has also been suggested some perfumes contain chemicals that imitate human pheromones, a secreted or excreted chemical known to trigger a response in other humans and, in this instance, to encourage sexual attention. Whether this is true, or whether it is a hypothesis propounded by the perfume industry to encourage greater sales—as is evident in many advertising campaigns—remains open to question, not least because too little is known about the human reaction to pheromones.

A brief history

Whatever the rationale for its existence, scent has certainly been around for a long time. The word perfume derives from the Latin "per fumum," meaning "through smoke," which indicates just how old is this form of personal enhancement and also its original nature. For millennia before Christianity, fragrant woods and resins would be burnt during religious ceremonies as a form of homage to pagan deities; even today in the West, some Roman Catholic services incorporate a thurible, a metal vessel suspended on a chain in which incense is burned. And aromatic incense continues to be used in Hindu, Buddhist, and Taoist ceremonies.

At some point, it was decided that instead of burning fragrance we should wear it ourselves, using oils and resins derived from natural substances, which, when coming into contact with body heat, would exude their inherent perfume. This practice was widespread among Egyptians and then passed to the Greeks and Romans, who would anoint themselves with scent after bathing. It also became common practice to perfume a corpse before burial, although perhaps this was to counter the odor of decay, especially in warm climates. Many of the items we still associate with fragrance, like glass bottles and pots, were first produced in large quantities during the same period. Fragrances were taken from flowers like irises and roses, plants such as sandalwood and mint, and even spices like cinnamon. These were crushed and blended with pure oils before application.

Following the collapse of the Roman Empire in Western Europe from the 5th century onward, interest in perfume was superseded by other concerns, most of them to do with basic survival. Further east, the Arabs developed the art of perfume making, refining the process of manufacture of fragrant oils and also perfumed waters. A key development was the discovery by the 11th-century Persian chemist and philosopher Ibn Sina, otherwise known as Avicenna, of how to extract essential oils from flowers and plants by means of steam distillation. The whole system of aromatherapy could not exist without his pioneering work in this field.

Perfume supposedly acts as a magnet for women, but anyone who has smelled somebody drenched in an unpleasantly powerful scent will argue otherwise

Some of Avicenna's voluminous writings on many subjects including medicine and health were translated into European languages. His process of perfume distillation was also adopted and formed the basis of all production until relatively recently. It was during the Renaissance period that perfume wearing once more became widespread, especially in Italy. When the Florentine Catherine de Medici married Henri II of France in 1533, she brought with her a personal perfumer, and his presence in Paris led to the city becoming a center of fragrance creation and manufacture, a status it has retained ever since. Likewise, the cultivation of flowers, essential for the extraction of their oils, became a major industry in the south of the country: the town of Grasse continues to be renowned in this regard.

Perfume wearing, among the affluent, was widespread for centuries, not least because it masked other, less savory smells. Napoleon Bonaparte, he who once wrote requesting his wife Josephine not to wash as he would be home in three days, had two quarts of violet cologne delivered to him each week and, in addition, went through 60 bottles of double extract of jasmine monthly. Evidently there was little of our modern distinction between fragrances deemed suitable for men and those for women. This was a development of the 19th century when perfume production became more commercial in response to the rise of a middle-class market. Whereas, hitherto, perfume had been the preserve of wealthy elites, now it started to enjoy a broader appeal. Around the same time, advances in chemistry made it possible to re-create natural scents with man-made materials. The modern perfume industry was born.

The science of scent

Perfumery is both an art and a science, and creators of scents, known as "noses," need to combine the knowledge of a scientist with the creativity of an artist. A great deal has been written about perfumes, much of it as likely to induce queasiness as a cheap scent. However, if you want to learn more on the subject, finding informative texts is not difficult. But be warned: discussions about perfume are like those about wine, not least because both attract opinionated bores.

In an effort to hold your attention, here is a synopsis of the various key facts you should know.

Like wine, perfume is composed of a sequence of "notes," which reveal themselves sequentially. Just as the wine in your mouth has an immediate taste, so too perfume has a top note, which is what you smell first. It rarely lasts more than a matter of minutes as the middle notes emerge, only to be supplanted in turn by the base notes—the core of the fragrance and the scent that you are going to smell in the hours ahead. Therefore, when you try a new fragrance in a department store or pharmacy, bear in mind that your immediate response to it will last no longer than do those top notes. You need to let the fragrance sit on your skin for some time before a full appreciation of it will be achieved.

Because there are now so many different fragrances on the market, they are usually divided into six groups, each with its own characteristics. Of these, floral is most popular with women but least with men because the latter associate it with the former: unlike Napoleon, today's man prefers not to douse himself in essence of jasmine. So-called Oriental scents are heavy and rich, with the evidence of spices and resins in their perfume. While they appeal to some men, they tend not to enjoy broad popularity. Citrus, on the other hand, which is tangy and refreshing with the zest of lime, lemon, and mandarin, does draw a broad constituency. So, too, do fragrances belonging to the fougère and chypre groups, since both have a mossy aroma. Fougère scents are inclined to be lighter, and chypre denser, but both are liked by men, as are green scents, which, as the name implies, tend to give the impression of natural freshness.

The higher the concentrations of perfume, the longer lasting the fragrance

In case all that was insufficiently complicated, it must be explained that fragrances also come in different strengths, depending on the concentration of pure perfume they contain. Eau de parfum, or EDP, has between eight and 15 percent pure fragrance, while eau de toilette (EDT) has four to five percent. Aftershave and eau fraîche are lighter still, with anything between one and three percent pure perfume. Stronger scents are more expensive because the ingredients cost more. On the other hand, the higher the concentration of perfume, the longer lasting the fragrance. You get what you pay for.

Selecting a fragrance

Deciding what scent suits you best is a matter of trial and error. Of course, it's not obligatory: if you don't want to wear any fragrance at all, that's your prerogative. Some men think of themselves as incomplete without a fragrance, whereas plenty of others have never used one. But, having made the decision to wear some kind of scent, you should proceed the easiest way, which is to choose first which group you like best, be it chypre, citrus, or whatever. Then look at what's on offer within this field. Even so, there is such a bewildering variety of options available, it is not difficult to become overwhelmed. So another simplification is to stick with classics and let the sound, good taste of many other men help you: go for scents that have proven their appeal over previous decades. Manufacturers bring out new products

every season, but few of them will stand the test of time. In fact, one of the hazards of selecting a new fragrance is precisely that it may be discontinued next year. A scent with a long history of success is more likely to remain in production and still be for sale long into the future.

As already advised, when you try a scent do bear in mind that it will smell different an hour or two after settling on the skin. So don't buy something just because you like how it smells immediately. Apply the fragrance on clean skin, ideally straight after bathing or showering, and then let it settle. If you're still happy with the smell later in the day, then most likely this is the right fragrance.

There are certain key places where you should apply product, namely on the wrists, behind the ears, and on the neck; the skin is thin at these points and the fragrance will be more quickly absorbed. Don't overdo it: scent should complement your natural body aroma, not overwhelm it and every other smell within a range of several miles. Take into account that some people possess a more acute sense of smell than others, and some are even allergic to modern scents, owing to the use of chemicals in their production. Be moderate in the application of any scent so that its presence is subtly apparent.

Finally, learn the value of loyalty, and make one scent distinctively your own. All of us possess a Proustian memory for smells, whether it is the aroma of particular meals we associate with childhood or the scent of someone we once loved. Wear the same fragrance for long enough and you will come to possess it in the minds of those who know you: every time they smell that scent, it will bring you to mind. This is the specific power of perfume, and it can be yours, too.

 # Men's cosmetics

In certain cultures and during certain periods men wore makeup, and sometimes just as much of it as women. The difference between the sexes did not extend to cosmetics: there are no stories of the ancient Egyptians dividing shades of eyeliner between boys and girls. Probably the last time men in any number wore makeup was the 18th century, although frequently this was to disguise or distract attention from skin problems such as pock marks caused by small pox. Come the 19th century, makeup for men fell out of favor as a more severe, and natural, look was preferred.

And that pretty much remains the case to the present day. Although there are periodic media stories about male cosmetics increasing in popularity, invariably these refer to skincare products like moisturizer rather than lipstick or mascara. Occasionally, someone in the public spotlight breaks ranks: ever since '70s shock rocker Alice Cooper, there have been musicians who decide to wear eyeliner in the hope of being noticed. This duly happens, and then they are ignored again. The fact is that for the past 200 years men have been discouraged from wearing makeup. As a rule, it is deemed effeminate and excessively vain, two traits the average man hopes he will never be accused of having.

Nevertheless, apparently more and more men are using cosmetics, albeit without ever declaring they do so publicly. The results of a survey released in January 2013 by online discount company HushHush.com showed that of more than 1,800 men polled, 11 percent admitted to wearing makeup, with over half that number doing so regularly, and one in five on a daily basis.

A little further investigation revealed precisely what these men were using, with 71 percent opting for concealer in order to hide skin blemishes or signs of tiredness under the eyes. Next in popularity came eyeliner and lipgloss, followed by mascara, although one suspects the number of men who wield a mascara brush with confidence is relatively small. The other popular item among

men, as indicated by this and other similar surveys, is self-tan. More than a third of those in the HushHush.com poll said they used such a product, although some two-thirds of them preferred to do the job at home, with the rest prepared to be given a spray tan at a salon.

Aside from that rather startling statistic about eyeliner (49 per cent apparently), what these figures make clear is that when a man uses cosmetics, he intends them to enhance rather than alter his natural appearance. A tan is judged indicative of good health and considered attractive, whereas acne spots or bags under the eyes imply the reverse. Therefore one is added and the other hidden from view.

A recent survey revealed that of more than 1,800 men polled, 11 percent admitted to wearing makeup

Concealers are certainly not to be eschewed. Applied with dexterity, they will do much to improve how you look on those days when you're suffering from sleep-deprivation or an unexpected outbreak of blemishes. They come in a variety of shades, so the first thing is to find that closest to your own skin tone and then employ with a deft hand. Just a little should do the trick: you're trying to conceal a problem, not bury it. Too much concealer will only draw attention to the blemish you intend to hide, so go easy for best results.

With regard to tans, although considered a sign of health, it is also now known that darkening your skin through exposure to the sun is liable to lead to cancer. Hence the popularity of fake tans, which mimic the real thing but without the inherent risks of overexposure to the sun.

If you decide to go down the route of fake tan, it is best to follow a couple of simple rules. First, set aside a bit of time and practice once or twice before your tan makes its public debut. Look around your supermarket or pharmacy and you will see plenty of possible products: choose one that is best for your skin type and is not too far removed from your present skin tone. The tan should be sheer, so that it is like a veil on your skin, and light so that your pores are not clogged. Remember that men's skin is thicker and coarser than that of women and so anything other than the finest tan will leave a residue.

We have all seen people who look more tangerine than tan, due to excessive use of a faking product

While coating your face with a layer of artificial tan does not require much skill, achieving good, even results on the rest of your body is much harder. You are quite likely to end up with parts of your anatomy featuring different shades. While your knees could be quite dark, for example, the area below them might still be pale or streaked like a piece of cheap bacon. Hair on your limbs makes fake tan harder to apply, as does our failure to have sufficiently long arms to reach the middle of our backs. A fake tan is best applied by a professional, who does this for a living and is therefore skilled at the task (and can be held responsible if the results are unsatisfactory). The sensible course of action is to visit a salon and have the job done properly.

Secondly, and just as important, whether on your face or anywhere else, choose a shade that looks natural. We have all

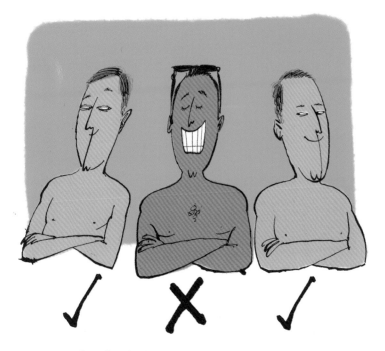

seen people who look more tangerine than tan, due to excessive use of a faking product. Tempted though you may be to convey the impression of six months basking in the Bahamas, the probability is that everyone knows you were desk-bound in an office during the same period of time. The phrase "sun-kissed" is often used to describe a good tan. Interpret that to mean a friendly peck on the cheek, not a blazing smooch.

In other words, when it comes to fake tan, don't get carried away. Here, as in so many other areas of life, less is best. In fact, follow the same rule with regard to all aspects of makeup: operate with a sure but light hand.

Chapter 8

Diet and Exercise

Yet again, it was that indefatigable wordsmith St. Paul who first proposed the idea that our bodies are temples: he mentioned this in a letter to the Corinthians, so perhaps the Greek city's residents were particularly overweight. Whatever the case, his quote has resonated over the centuries, not least because many of us are aware that our own temples have become run down with age, or started to bulge at the external walls. Eventually we reach the point where a thorough program of restoration will be needed if the temple is to get back into decent condition.

Diet

The ideal, of course, is ongoing maintenance rather than radical repair work. And one way to ensure your temple stays in good shape is to watch what you eat and drink. This becomes steadily more the case as we age. According to the American Dietetic Association, older men find it more difficult to keep down their weight due to a combination of decreasing lean body mass and increasing slothfulness. When young, we are full of energy and are therefore able to burn up a lot of calories. We engage with physical exercise and require an abundance of food to replenish our vitality. With the passage of time, however, our lives are inclined to become more static and our bodies less responsive to exertion. At the same time, our intake of food and drink remains the same or even increases, with the inevitable result that we put on weight.

So the first lesson to be learned is that, from around the age of 30, we should consider eating both less and with greater care if our waistband is not to grow. A 2010 study published in the *Journal of the American Medical Association* revealed that over 70 percent of men in the United States were either overweight or obese, with negative consequences for their general health and longevity prospects. A measure called the Body Mass Index (BMI) is commonly used to determine an individual's body fat based on weight and height. You can easily conduct this test on yourself, finding the relevant information on the internet. If your BMI is over 25, then you are deemed to be overweight, if over 30, obese.

Men are more likely to suffer from both these conditions than women for the same reason they are vulnerable to other health issues: failure to tackle the problem combined with an attitude peculiar to their gender, namely the irrational belief that ignoring an issue will lead to successful resolution. As a result, the numbers of overweight and obese men in Western society has grown, accompanied by a corresponding rise in certain conditions such as diabetes and heart disease.

Men diagnosed as suffering from one or both of these

complaints are liable to find themselves advised on the importance of changing their diets. You can avoid reaching that point by watching what you eat and drink, and by keeping tabs on both the quality and quantity of your consumption. While some foods are better for us than others, nothing should be taken in excess. Moderation in all things must be your rule.

From the age of 30 we should consider eating less and with greater care if our waistband is not to grow

Food and drink are composed of a number of elements in different combinations: carbohydrates, proteins, fats, and vitamins and minerals. We need all of them to stay healthy but not equal measures of all. As the name indicates, carbohydrates contain carbon, hydrogen, and oxygen and are required by the body to produce energy. Derived from cereals, pulses, vegetables, and fruit, they include sugars and starch and are broken down in the body to form glucose. You need to be careful about your intake of carbohydrates because any glucose surplus to immediate requirements is stored in the liver and muscles as glycogen, which can potentially lead to diabetes.

Proteins have a similar composition to carbohydrates but with the addition of nitrogen. Found in meat, fish, dairy products, and eggs, protein can also be derived from some cereals and beans. It is necessary to us to enable growth, development, and repair of our bodies, as well as the production of enzymes, like those used for digestion, and hormones. Although often frowned upon, fats, also called lipids, are essential to your wellbeing. Found in meat, fish, and vegetable oils, fat is used to build nerves and the brain (40 percent of the latter is fat), insulate the body, produce hormones and cholesterol, and perform sundry other functions. Obtained from a variety of foodstuffs, vitamins and minerals are substances essential to ensure good health.

Eating healthily

And so to the specifics of your diet. First, a handful of rules you must follow without fail. Always eat a decent breakfast, and never skip it on the grounds of having insufficient time. Breakfast is the most important meal of the day and sets you up for what lies ahead. There is an old saying that we should breakfast like kings, lunch like princes, and dine like paupers. Even if you're anti-royalist, this makes excellent sense since it takes into account our body's metabolism and the process of burning calories through activity. In other words, consuming the largest amount of food at the start of the day and the least at its conclusion is the most beneficial approach. It is also essential that you eat three meals regularly, and around the same time each day, not just because you need the energy but also because setting up habitual patterns of behavior of this sort ensures you are less likely to snack. Your body responds well to consistency, and will not crave sustenance at odd hours if it is used to a daily intake of food on the same three occasions. Finally, try to eat something from every food group during each meal, because that way you are more likely to have a balanced diet.

That ideal balanced diet is most often known by the generic name of the Mediterranean Diet, based on the idea that it is

consumed by peoples living around the periphery of the sea of the same name. Whether this is true or not, the main feature of the Mediterranean Diet is that it contains only moderate quantities of fat but a high intake of fruit and vegetables, whole grains, nuts, and seeds. It also features sufficient quantities of "good" fats known to be kind to the heart and arteries, such as olive and canola oil. Finally, while the Mediterranean Diet includes a reasonable amount of fish and poultry each week, it only allows for the consumption of red meat on a few occasions each month. Much of this food is rich in minerals and vitamins, low in calories, and high in fiber. In other words, it contains all the benefits of healthy eating, while leaving you feeling replete.

Not only will you keep down your weight by following a variant of the Mediterranean Diet, you will also reduce the possibility of suffering other illnesses such as heart disease and even some cancers.

Foods to avoid

By now, anyone with even a modicum of education will be aware that we ought to eat food as close to its raw condition as possible and shun refined foods like sugars. So you should steam vegetables rather than have them fried, and opt for fresh fruit over chocolate. While we need a certain amount of carbohydrates daily to provide us with sufficient energy for physical activity and cognitive function, we ought not to overdo it since carbohydrates also elevate blood-sugar levels, and not all of them are metabolized into energy. The Institute of Medicine in the United States recommends adults should receive 45–65 percent of dietary energy from carbohydrates, while the World Health Organization, in 2003, proposed a figure of 55–75 percent but recommended only ten percent of this come from sugars. On average it is proposed that carbohydrates make up 55 percent of your daily diet, fats 30 percent, and protein 15 percent.

Approach a lifestyle transformation slowly and make the changes at a leisurely pace

The rules are not difficult, but nor are the reasons we fail to follow them: laziness, self-indulgence, a fondness for salt, fat, and sugar, and an erroneous belief that we are going to live forever. The last of these takes a blow first when we find it hard to run up even a short flight of steps without losing our breath, soon after which we are diagnosed with a serious coronary condition.

If this happens to you, then your doctor will most likely insist on a change in eating habits. Even without medical intervention, many men decide to alter their food consumption for the better. Opting for this season's fashionable diet is not recommended; many of them emphasize one food group at the expense of others, and also insist on too extreme an approach. Unless you have exceptional will power, you are liable to find shedding all your bad practices at the same time an enterprise impossible to sustain. Most likely you will fall back into the old ways: your health and waistline will not have improved, and nor your mood (or indeed your pocket since dieting plans always seem to require additional expenditure).

Approach a lifestyle transformation slowly and make the changes at a leisurely pace. Gradually shed the bad foods and adopt those known to be good for you. That way you will find it easier to keep going. While results might not appear as fast as you would wish, odds-on they will be permanent. It takes a while for body and mind alike to grow accustomed to a new regime, so don't rush things. And make sure to allow yourself an occasional reward: eating should be a pleasure, not a punishment.

What to drink

Obviously, all the previous information and advice also apply to your consumption of liquids. About 60 percent of our body is made up of water. Some of this is lost every day as we flush out toxins through bowel movements and urine, perspiration, and even breath. So it must be replenished if we are not to suffer from dehydration, which, in turn, leads to want of energy and lassitude. Some of this liquid we receive through food, but the greater part of it will be in the form of drinks. The American Institute of Medicine has determined that an adequate intake of liquid for each day is three liters, which works out at about 13 cups.

The greater part of this should be taken as plain water. However, we also consume other liquids, most frequently tea, coffee, various sugared drinks, and alcohol. These can have

positive effects, at least in the short term and in temperate quantities. Coffee, for example, acts as a stimulant, thanks to the presence of caffeine, and sometimes we require this in order to function, particularly when feeling tired. Similarly, a glass of wine with your meal can not only aid digestion but also lower the risk of heart disease, stroke, and diabetes.

As with food, what matters most is that you engage with all forms of drink with full awareness that moderation is best. One glass of wine may be good but that does not mean two glasses is better and three even more beneficial. Limit your intake of all liquids other than plain water, not least because, as a rule, they contain minimal nutrients. If you find yourself growing overly fond of, or dependent on, any of them, then it is best to wean yourself off entirely.

Exercise

No matter how good your diet, it will only be of limited benefit if not combined with some kind of exercise regime. The concept of exercise, as we understand it, is of relatively recent origin. Until the Industrial Revolution of the 19th century, the majority of men engaged in manual labor every day of their lives, mostly working in agriculture, in order to produce sufficient food for survival. Physical exertion was an inherent part of this process and therefore many of our forebears suffered from the consequences of too much, rather than too little exercise.

Exercise requires effort, both physical and mental, and the second of these is just as critical as the first

Our bodies evolved over millennia in the expectation that daily toil would be their lot. Now, however, the average male is no longer sweating in the fields but, instead, leads a sedentary existence. As a result, it is essential we put our bodies through their paces in some other way if they are not to undergo rapid degeneration through lack of use. Hence the importance of exercise.

Just as most of us don't relish the idea of plowing or picking root vegetables, so we are disinclined to approach exercise with delight. Mankind is inherently indolent, and it is important to understand and accept this fact. Exercise requires effort, both physical and mental, and the second of these is just as critical as the first. Other than full-time sportsmen, few of us regard physical activity with relish. On the other hand, once we have embarked on even a short bout of exercise, we are likely to feel better. Scientific research has shown that exertion increases levels of endorphins and serotonin in the brain, both of which play a part in establishing our sense of well-being. Furthermore, rises in

core body temperature and increased blood flow to the brain, both of which occur during exercise, trigger mood improvement. Finally, although less easy to monitor, it is widely accepted that regular exercise leads to better self-image and greater confidence, which, in turn, is advantageous to our mental health. There is also research indicating that exercise promotes better sleep: all of us know that when we are physically tired, we fall asleep quicker and remain asleep longer than on those occasions when we haven't stirred from the sofa all day. In other words, while we may be temperamentally reluctant to embark on exercise, once this barrier is overcome we immediately experience the advantages, not least psychological.

Research indicates that exercise promotes a better night's sleep

Although we are usually aware of the importance of exercise and know we will look and feel better for engaging in physical activity, nevertheless we remain reluctant to do so. The problem is that, in our culture, exercise has come to be represented as extreme activity and, accordingly, appears unappealing, especially at the onset. According to British government statistics, only 37 percent of men take sufficient exercise to derive any benefit from it, with consequences for the health of the nation. Surely at least part of the explanation for this low number is the way in which exercise is usually characterized as some kind of demanding challenge that will leave us feeling debilitated.

Keep it simple

On the contrary, it is perfectly possible to reach the required quota of exercise without too much effort. Adult males should engage in a minimum of 30 minutes moderate-to-reasonably-intense physical activity at least five days a week. This means you must feel at least some sense of exertion and increased body warmth, but not that you are draped over a gym weight machine gasping for breath and dripping sweat. A brisk walk will do the trick, as will climbing stairs (as opposed to taking the elevator) or cycling (as opposed to taking the bus). Even better, the 30 minutes do not need to follow each other consecutively: as long as you spend at least that much time each day in exercise, even if broken into smaller units of five or ten minutes, then you will enjoy all the rewards. If you are seriously out of shape, diagnosed as obese, or deemed at risk from conditions such as diabetes, then the amount of time required to be spent exercising is likely to increase, rising to a minimum of one hour each day. Yet again this is proof of the advantages of keeping yourself in good condition.

As we grow older it becomes still more critical that exercise has a daily place in our lives. Remaining in good physical condition renders us better able to look after ourselves and not be dependent on others. It is also clear that elderly people who are physically healthy are more likely to be mentally in good shape, too. If you want to live long and well, sloth is not to be considered.

How to enjoy exercising

Should you plan to embark on an exercise regime more strenuous than a daily walk, then bear in mind the following key points.

* Choose an activity that you are most likely to enjoy. There's no point torturing yourself with long-distance marathons if you hate running even to catch a train. Some forms of exercise are understandably more popular than others, like cycling or swimming. Not only do these improve your state of health but they do so in a way that is relatively undemanding.

* Pace yourself. If you haven't undertaken any exercise for a long time, then start slowly. Set yourself achievable goals and gradually build up to them: once they're reached, you can always give yourself a greater challenge. Don't be unrealistic about what's possible; it takes time to get fit and, especially if you are past your twenties, your body will no longer be able to do as much as once might have been the case.

* Wear appropriate clothing. An obvious tip you might think, but an astonishing number of people don't understand that the clothes they wear every day to work are not suited for exercise. In particular, invest in a pair of decent sports shoes, which will give your feet

the support they need when engaging in physical activity. Inappropriate footwear can put unnecessary strain on other parts of your body, not least your knees and back, with the threat of consequent injury.

* Consider joining a group or club, or even starting one. Many of us, when we decide to get into shape, think of the enterprise as a solitary activity. On the contrary, there are plenty of exercise regimes that depend on a number of participants: you could join a local soccer group, for example. One of the advantages to doing something like this is that the other members act as a spur to ensuring you remain committed. It's easy to put off exercise when this involves a solitary run in the winter rain but harder when the rest of the team is waiting for you to turn up.

Exercise becomes less burdensome and more fun when it is participatory, and when there's a social element to the experience. For the same reason, if you take up swimming or cycling or even walking, look for local groups engaging in the activity. Most public swimming pools, for example, have classes for a number of people at a time. The hardship of exercise won't seem so bad when the experience is shared with other people.

You could, of course, opt for working out in a gym. Our ancestors would surely be first baffled and then amused by establishments where the clientele pay money to engage in physical toil. And, indeed, it remains somewhat extraordinary that, with so many forms of exercise available free, the

most obvious being a daily walk, large numbers of people decide instead to be charged for the same thing. Obviously gyms have equipment and facilities that you most likely will not have at home, whether weight machines or a swimming pool. Many of these devices allow you to build up and improve the musculature of certain parts of your body, and there are instructors to supervize you while doing so. This is their unique selling point and one that enjoys widespread popularity. So if you do wish to bulk up your arms or chest or legs or all of them and more besides, then a gym is to be recommended.

There is another advantage to gyms, even if not one intended by their owners: having spent money on membership fees, you are more likely to turn up and use the facilities than would be the case if you were embarking on a free regime. That, at least, is the theory. Ten years ago, however, a survey in Britain discovered the drop-out rate for gyms was 80 percent. In other words, four out of five people, having paid membership fees—which are usually quite substantial—then opted not to take advantage of the facilities on which they had spent money. If ever there was evidence of our reluctance to engage with exercise, it comes from this statistic. Also apparent is the fact that spending money cannot automatically be equated with improving your health or physique: if this were the case, we could all choose to be poor but fit. We would then be just like the majority of our ancestors, except they had no choice in the matter. Such are the vagaries of human nature.

Index